Secrets of A Business Broker

A Real Life Journey and No BS Playbook For Buying A Business

Written By Alex Khabbaz

Managing Partner @ Texas Business Brokers

4 Successful Exits — 10+ Years Selling Businesses

With commentary By Warren Baas, SBA Lending Expert

Secrets of A Business Broker
A Real-Life Journey and No-BS Playbook for Buying a Business

PUBLISHER & IMPRINT INFORMATION
Published by Texas Business Brokers Press
Austin, Texas, USA
www.texasbusinessbrokers.com

CREDITS
Written and Designed by Alex Khabbaz
Interior Formatting & Typesetting by Alex Khabbaz
Lender Commentary by Warren Baas

ISBN & PUBLICATION DATA ISBN: 979-8-9976564-1-6 (Paperback)
ISBN: 978-8-9976564-2-3 (Hardcover)
ISBN: 978-8-9976564-0-9 (eBook)
First Edition: 2026

Acknowledgement | And Sincere Thanks

Writing this book has been as much a process of deep self-reflection as it has been a professional endeavor. I am profoundly grateful to the many people who stood by me through my "reality checks", went completely above and beyond their duties, and gently redirected me to the right path. Without you, I could not have done this any other way.

To my wife, Tara: You have been my absolute rock. Thank you for sticking by me and picking me up when I was down, even when I screwed up royally, for always encouraging me to take risks, and not settling for anything but my best.

To David Kelley: Most importantly, thank you for basically adopting me when I was just eight years old. By caring for me and introducing me to entrepreneurship at the age of thirteen, you planted the seeds that changed the entire trajectory of my life. I owe you a debt of gratitude that can never be fully repaid.

To my mentor, business partner, and brother, Mike: Thank you for teaching me the true complexities of selling businesses and for your invaluable guidance over the past 12 years. Your professional wisdom and personal friendship have truly been a blessing.

To the "Grumpy Old Men": To the retired CEOs who took a young guy under their wing during the wild days of Rainboxx—thank you for your time and executive mentorship. A very special, intentional shoutout to **Rod Conard**, who went above and beyond to mentor me on the side and teach me how to truly think like a successful leader.

To Ryan Guthrie: Thank you for teaching me the ropes and helping me design and build my very first website back in 2010 for Austex Sprinklers. You gave me the digital edge I needed when the rest of the industry was still using a physical Rolodex.

To Gary Kulp: My friend and former boss—thank you for always taking the time to build me up, believe in my potential, and consistently provide me with meaningful, positive advice when I needed it most.

To the many rest: To my brother Sam, my uncle Camille, "HuKaBut" family and my step-father—thank you for your quiet support, your guidance, and for being structural pillars in my life when I needed guidance or love.

And Most Importantly, to my Lord and Savior, Jesus Christ

Table of Contents

Chapter 1 | Reality Check

It was 2014 when I woke up from a power nap after a long day of day-drinking. The only problem was that I had chosen to take that nap at a Murphy's Gas Station, and I had thrown up on myself.

Thankfully, the police officer who politely woke me up knocking on my window was pretty grossed out and decided not to take me to jail. Instead, he made the call to my wife to pick me up. Sitting there, I am pretty sure I would have preferred jail that night.

At that moment, and during the painfully sobering day that followed, I experienced a massive reality check, and I am incredibly grateful that I did. It was the turning point in my life when I finally realized that money does not make you happy. I had a beautiful family, a thriving business, a home, and everything society says you need to be fulfilled. Yet, there I was, waking up covered in my own vomit at a gas station.

That was the day I decided to sell my first business and fundamentally reevaluate how I was doing life. Since then, I have had four successful exits, built one of the most successful business brokerages in the state of Texas, and found true happiness through the grace of God. I still casually drink—but I needed that brutal reality check to truly understand that a profound change was necessary.

I am writing this book primarily for two reasons:

> First, just like myself who needed a few reality checks and guidance to find the right path to success, there are countless buyers out there needing the same and don't even know it and a lot of whom have no idea why they are failing to acquire a business.
>
> Second, I have grown weary of the so-called "experts" and advisors leading good people astray with terrible advice and making it seem so easy when it's not.

I will use my proven **SELL SIDE** experience as a successful Business Broker to provide you with accurate and actionable guidance on how to successfully buy a business.

False Teachings

Whether we like it or not, our lives are built on a foundation of some kind. For most of my life, my foundation was built on a complete lie that I inherited. My family moved to the U.S. in 1979 from Beirut, Lebanon, where they had enjoyed power, fame, and wealth. But all of that soon faded. The trauma of war, arranged marriages, and a gambling problem led to the rapid downfall of a once-prominent, proud family.

I was raised in a single-parent household in Burbank, California, by a mother who suffered from trauma induced mental illness. Her worldview was shaped by trauma, and she placed all of her self-worth and value in looks and wealth. Naturally, I became a product of my upbringing valuing the wrong things. I bought into the lie that money would solve my problems and make me happy.

As you already know, that was not the case. I was doing life wrong. Heck, I am still messing up regularly - just ask my wife—but I became self-aware enough to realize that my methods and the way I was viewing things were flawed.

Just as I was taught a poor foundation of values and didn't know it until I was about 27 years old, the same goes for inspiring entrepreneurs looking to buy a business. If you have been in the market to buy a business and you keep coming up empty-handed, it is time for you to look in the mirror and acknowledge the same thing: **your acquisition methods are the problem and wrong.**

Why You Should (Or Shouldn't) Listen to Me

One of the biggest issues buyers face is the epidemic of fake experts and text book advice from those so called experts. It is important to truly verify the individual or group you are taking advice from. My recommendation is to verify that an expert's claimed experience is legitimate and applicable to the type of transaction you are likely seeking. For example, when they say they bought or sold 200 companies, was it a passive investment of 1% or controlling share? Did they start the business and sell it or were they just a part of a tech buyout as an employee?

My first piece of advice to achieve success is to get details and verify what you are told. That saying "Trust but verify" has value. Investigate the people giving you advice. Make sure they truly have the skills to guide you. Don't just believe them because they have money or are flashy and be careful on how they define or present their experience.

Heck, be wary of me, too. Why should you listen to a guy who couldn't control his alcohol and allegedly, is terrible at karaoke (I respectfully beg to differ on the karaoke).

Well, you should listen to me because this "mess-up" has had four successful exits selling his own businesses (two started from ground up and two as a partner), and has been the sell-side broker for many Main Street businesses through a reputable firm that thrives today (Texas Business Brokers). I urge you to go online now and read the reviews from real people who have worked with me or my firm.

The advice you are going to get in these pages that follow comes straight from a source with direct, verifiable sell-side experience. By the end of this book, you will know the exact process and strategy to successfully buy a QUALITY business (fyi, the businesses you don't want are always available).

Chapter 2 | Not All Advisors are Good Advisors

The Epidemic of Fake Experts

I was 18 years old when I first started realizing that some things aren't what they appear to be. At the time, I got a job as a teller at Wells Fargo in Seattle. I had the opportunity to cash a lot of checks, perform deposits, help with withdrawals, and most importantly, sign people up for online banking, which was cutting-edge tech for the time.

Wow, that was a long time ago.

Anyways, to get to the point, I saw a lot of bank accounts. The people you would think to be the wealthiest by presentation, ie nice suits, jewelry, name brand clothes, super confident, sometimes arrogant and so forth, usually had the least amount of money in their accounts.

The people I least expected, however, had the most. They would not stand out. Most of them almost appeared poor or lazy about their appearance. There were outliers, but the majority of the time, the flashier they were, or the more they bragged, the less they had.

Writing this, I think this is still true today. I work with a lot of successful business owners, and the ones making the most, usually don't have Porsches or come off flashy. So, be careful not to fall into the illusion trap. Just because someone shows off wealth or says they are an expert, doesn't mean they are.

Just like those flashy bank customers who were secretly broke, the internet is currently flooded with Fake Experts or so called "business gurus". These fake experts, who sell services on how to buy a business, typically offer textbook advice from a buyer's perspective that doesn't survive in real world applications for main street $5m or less business acquisitions.

Additionally, some of those "Business Gurus" are simply great marketers, phrasing their experience in ways that present them as experts in acquisition, and selling a unattainable dream to a hopeful buyer who wants to better their lives.

Simply put, the biggest reason Buyers are not seeing success is that the foundation of what you know or being taught is built on bad or outdated advice by individuals who lack true direct industry experience.

The biggest lie is everything you see on Social Media. I see brilliant marketers who have built cult-like followings. They use great marketing, fancy imaging, and generic information found online to give advice and sell a dream. Their advice and textbook teaching aren't always 100% wrong, but it rarely survives contact with the real world of small business acquisitions.

Note From The Lender's Desk By Warren Baas

Stop paying thousands of dollars to online influencers before you get a free pre-qualification from an actual lender. I regularly see searchers who fall down a social media rabbit hole, get hooked on the "no-money-down" myth, and waste $7,000 to $15,000 on an unnecessary flashy mastermind or cohort. It's a waste of money!

I am not saying those individuals were never successful or don't have something to offer; they just don't have the right experience to teach what you need to succeed in buying a business.

I have found great success as an entrepreneur, and to be clear, I am not trying to say I am better at being an entrepreneur than them. Heck, I'm not buying all of Elon Musk's shares in Tesla anytime soon, or ringing the bell at the New York Stock Exchange. I am simply a man who built a beautiful life with a level of financial freedom that is truly attainable by anyone. Not everyone can be Elon Musk, but everyone can achieve what I have achieved: financial independence, quality time with family, and true peace. All I am trying to say is they don't have the right experience, and their teachings are making them a lot of money and setting inspiring buyers up for failure, probably unknowingly. IF IT SEEMS TO BE TOO GOOD TO BE TRUE AND EASY, TREAD CAREFULLY.

Note From The Lender's Desk

Don't mistake an "experts" ability to acquire stakes in businesses as true acquisition knowledge or operating knowledge in a business. There have been deals I funded where an influencer owned a 5% or less stake; and absolutely counted it in their portfolio and told a success story about the business…sometimes the partner will be mentioned, plenty of times not.

Here are two ways you can spot a marketing expert: Look at the math and ask yourself is this too good to be true?

If a so-called expert tells you they have bought 100 or 200 businesses, they are likely misleading you. What do they consider a business? A Shopify website? Are they counting the shares they buy in Amazon? (In that case, I've bought 500 businesses this year through my S&P 500 index funds!).

From my direct experience running a highly successful brokerage firm, I have personally sold plenty of businesses in ten plus years. The average business sale process takes 90 to 120 days from the Letter of Intent to Closing. Just buying 100 actual, operating businesses takes a very long time to just acquire them, let alone manage and resell them. If your "Expert" or "Advisor" isn't 90 years old, their claims should be heavily scrutinized.

The Corporate M&A Trap & Advisors

When I first started in the industry, I was told a saying, "Attorneys, Advisors, and CPA's kill deals". This is true to some extent. If you get an advisor, attorney, or CPA (or even business broker) who only works on one Business Acquisition or Sale a year, it's likely going to be a difficult process because they lack real-world everyday experience and will approach things in a black-and-white textbook manner, which leads to unnecessary conflicts.

Many "Experts" or "Advisors" coming from the Corporate world lean on their corporate M&A (Mergers & Acquisitions) experience. This experience is usually legitimate in boardrooms, but it is rarely applicable to sub-$5,000,000 transactions. When buying a $500,000, $1,000,000, or $3,000,000 business, you do not need advice on how to structure a $45,000,000 private equity buyout.

Being an entrepreneur who operates a local company is entirely different than being a CEO or an analyst at a corporate job. These corporate advisors rarely understand the Main Street landscape or what it takes to run a small business, which ultimately harms the buyers they advise.

My recommendation is to be open to Lender and Attorney referrals from sell-side brokers. Compare them to your advisors and verify that all advisors have proven, recurring experience in the specific service you need.

You don't want an Irrigation Specialist who occasionally works on roofs installing a brand new $40,000 roof for you. So why would you want a divorce attorney or a real estate agent who sells homes working on your M&A transaction, or similar?

Secret from the Broker's Desk

I am hesitant to work with buyers who have their own advisors, that is not a lender, business attorney, or CPA, particularly "Business Consultants" or "Business Advisor". Most advisors who don't fall into those buckets of experts, are usually a wrench in the transaction and profiting off your inexperience.

If I had two equal buyers, one who says they are using their own advisors, and another who doesn't but is open to referrals, I would always lean towards the buyer who is using my pre-qualified referrals and recommend to a seller that they choose that buyer over the other.

Chapter 3 | The Harsh Realities of the Market (and life for me)

If you want to win, you have to understand the reality of the battlefield.

Sadly, for a long time, I was completely clueless about the realities of adulthood. When I "graduated" high school in May 2003, I turned eighteen and became an adult overnight—well, at least legally. Mentally, I was either twenty-nine or twelve, depending on the scenario, but I didn't know that at the time. All I knew was that I was the smartest person in the room and had everything figured out, even though my actions contradicted that at every turn. I had absolutely zero self-awareness.

Guided by my self-declared genius, I had no real plan. So, I decided to join the Navy. In my mind, it was an easy way to buy myself some time before I had to figure out what I was actually doing with my life.

Needless to say, I fundamentally misunderstood the battlefield, the obligations, and the commitment I was making. I successfully got myself kicked out of the Navy during boot camp, and honestly, the Navy successfully dodged a bullet.

The commitment required was the exact opposite of the person I was at the time. Up until that point, I had operated with zero structure or stability in my life; I just did whatever I wanted. When I stepped off the bus at Great Lakes, Illinois for boot camp, I had no clue what I had gotten myself into. As the weeks passed, I was thriving in certain ways, but I couldn't understand why they did things the way they did. To my undisciplined mind, it just seemed inefficient. Plus, being told I had to work 12-hour days, stand watch, and couldn't party or hang out with girls meant my life was basically over. How could an eighteen-year-old idiot go on?

Luckily for both the Navy and me, we parted ways. I received a medical discharge for "failure to adapt"—which is the military's polite way of saying this kid is bat-shit crazy. Even more luckily, because it happened so early, it was an uncharacterized separation, not a dishonorable discharge, so it didn't ruin my permanent record. But the lesson was glaring: my lens on reality was completely skewed, and I was entirely incapable of seeing the world from any perspective other than my own.

I share this embarrassing story with you because acquiring a business is a battle you might not be ready for.

I have seen highly confident, historically successful buyers experience the exact same harsh reality check I had at Great Lakes. When they step onto the acquisition battlefield, they realize their corporate rules no longer apply. Some rise to the challenge, but others crumble under the weight of their own misconceptions.

Truly understanding what you are getting yourself into will help you decide whether acquiring a business is the right decision for you. I will share much more about the turbulent ups and downs of small business ownership later in this book, but first, you need to understand the realities of your first battle: the acquisition process.

The Supply vs. Demand Problem

There are many more qualified buyers than quality businesses available for purchase. Always. Many buyers step onto the battlefield entirely unaware of the intense competition they face. When a Business Broker lists a business for sale that is properly valued, they will receive a tremendous amount of inquiries. I routinely receive 50 plus inquiries in the first week alone for a good listing. It is critical for you to know this so you can act accordingly, set yourself apart, and significantly increase your chances of securing the deal. If you are difficult, unprepared, or arrogant, a broker will simply move to the next name on the list.

> 👁 **Note From The Lender's Desk**
>
> *I completely concur with Alex here, especially regarding the arrogance trap. I routinely speak with highly confident buyers who have consumed way more social media content about Entrepreneurship Through Acquisition (ETA) than they have actually looked at real live deals. They love to lecture me about how it's a "buyer's market" because of the heavily marketed "Silver Tsunami" of retiring business owners.*
>
> *Let's look at the actual reality on the ground: yes, there are approximately 36 million small businesses operating in the United States. But precious few of those are actually profitable, well-structured, or remotely worth buying. Spend more than three weeks actively searching for a quality company to acquire, and then come back and try to tell me about your hypothetical "buyer's market." The competition for healthy, cash-flowing assets is fierce. If you walk into a transaction acting entitled, you will get left behind.*

Complex Process

A lot of buyers think buying a business is like buying a home, however, that is far from accurate. Buying a business is 10x harder and requires grit and commitment. The process, once you're lucky enough to find a quality business, usually takes 90-120 days after the business goes under LOI.

A buyer will be working with banks, accountants, attorneys, and landlords negotiating contracts, getting approved for loans and leases, all while verifying the business they are buying is represented accurately with no liabilities.

The process is hard, and you need to learn to embrace the challenge because nothing good comes easy, however, I can promise that the reward in the end will be worth it.

Bad Brokers

I hear this time and time again, many brokers representing businesses are terrible to work with. I hear complaints that they misrepresent the businesses, are slow to respond, are inexperienced, and shouldn't have any business selling a business. The good news is that this book will teach you how to navigate an inexperienced or bad broker to successfully acquire a quality company if they got lucky enough to represent one.

> **Note From The Lender's Desk**
>
> *Here is a frightening reality check about the M&A industry: currently, only 18 states require business brokers to hold any kind of formal license—real estate or otherwise. That means in most of the country, literally any warm body can call themselves a business broker, and a massive amount of untrained people try. There is a severe shortage of legitimate, highly trained intermediaries in this space.*
>
> *To counter this, you will often see brokers with a massive string of letters trailing behind their names on email signatures and websites: CBI, CBB, M&AMI, CCIM, CFA, or even CPA. On paper, those titles are supposed to indicate a high level of rigorous, formal professional training, and they tell me as a lender that a particular broker really should know better. Yet, time and time again, the CIMs landing on my desk are incredibly sloppy, and the baseline financial diligence is completely lacking.*

FYI, being a business broker isn't easy on the emotions, and I see many brokers come and go. At times, I've thought about changing my profession. It's heartbreaking when you spend 6 months working on a listing, and the deal falls through a week before closing for something completely out of your control, or not knowing if your going to have a good or bad financial year income wise. A lot impacts business sales, such as COVID, international conflicts, interest rates, presidential campaigns, etc. So it's a roller coaster of a career even if you're good at it and make a lot of money doing it. Sometimes it feels like it's not worth it.

Costs

A lot of time, buyers assume the initial risks and costs of the acquisition process. I've seen buyers spend $20,000 to $30,000 on legal fees and deals fall apart. In most cases, these buyers don't take my advice and walk their own path, which ultimately hurts them, but even doing it correctly will require you to take some financial risk. Therefore, it's important to find a good quality seller who truly wants to sell. You don't want someone who is on the fence because they can just get cold feet and walk away without penalty. When that happens, you are out of any money you spent, and there is not much you can do about it.

The Clock is Ticking

Because buyers drastically underestimate the competition, they also underestimate the required speed they need to move at to be successful. Quality businesses do not stay on the market long. Usually, a great listing goes under contract within the first 30 days. You do not have weeks to leisurely ponder if you like the industry, or to wait around for your lawyer to return your calls. As a Buyer, you must review offerings the moment they are listed and move with aggressive precision until you secure exclusivity.

Broker Secrets: The Truth About Buyside Representation, Passive Income & Franchises

Why Buy-Side Representation is Dead

Many buyers look for a broker to represent them. The truth is, buy-side broker representation is virtually dead. If a broker is willing to offer buy-side representation, they are likely unsuccessful in sell-side representation, which is where the real money is earned. So, they are likely not in the elite class which locates and sells the few well-packed deals that come to market.

When a Broker works with a buyer, there usually is no way to guarantee they will make any money without taking money upfront since many buyers give up and never actually buy a business. This tends to occur for a number of reasons, such as simply getting discouraged, might not find a business they like, they might uncover issues in due diligence, they might get cold feet, the bank might deny their loan, etc.

Lastly, for every good business I list, there are 100x buyers available. Because of this, requesting to meet a busy broker for coffee or a "15-minute intro call" is an inefficient use of a broker's time. I receive multiple requests for coffee every week by “Serious” buyers assuming they are unique. So for many years, we offered zero Buyside Services.

The best way to build a relationship with a broker is to be highly prepared and responsive when they actually post a listing. If the deal doesn't work out for you, but you did everything right, the broker will remember you. When I recognize a name, I search my emails to see the past interactions. If they are positive, and everything still aligns, you have an automatic advantage. It shows you've been seriously looking for a period of time now.

Secret from the Broker's Desk

Let me be clear: I don't want to meet for coffee, and I don't care about your search criteria. The only way I will meet is through a paid consultation session, usually $750 for an hour. When that happens, I begin to care and take the buyer seriously. This proves they are serious and gives me the opportunity to help prepare them for the endeavor.

Note From The Lender's Desk

We experience the exact same sentiment on the banking side of the table. Lenders get hit up constantly by optimistic searchers wanting to "grab 20 minutes just to see if we're operationally aligned."

I always respond with a short, non-negotiable checklist, before I schedule a single minute on my calendar, I require a searcher to send over, at the very least, a completed SBA Personal Financial Statement (PFS), a professional resume, and a Personal Information Form. I sometimes struggle with having to screen people out using such an impersonal, rigid method, but if we don't protect our time, we will never get actual, impactful deal underwriting done. If you want a lender's time, bring your financial proof upfront.

The "Passive Income" Myth

If you are looking to buy a laundromat, a car wash, or an ATM route because you want "passive income," you are likely wasting your time. Have people bought laundromats and found success? Yes. Are the odds in your favor? No. Owning a business is difficult and is never truly 100% absentee.

The Franchise Trap

Regarding franchises, my advice is simple: be incredibly cautious. Unless you have the opportunity to acquire a Chick-fil-A or an absolute legacy brand, tread carefully.

At least once a month, I receive a call from a franchise owner who is desperately trying to sell. In almost all cases, their businesses are unsellable. They have lost money for years, or their cash flow is so minimal that they would be better off getting a job at a big-box retailer with benefits and less stress.

The structural flaw of most retail franchises is the high upfront cost, the long-term commercial lease, and the royalty structure. Franchisors take their percentage right off the top-line revenue, meaning you pay them whether you are profitable or bleeding cash.

If I had to choose between taking $50,000 to start a franchise or putting it on black at a roulette table, I would choose the roulette table. The odds of success are higher, and the loss is far less painful. Working 50 hours a week while losing thousands of dollars a month, trapped in a long-term lease, is a unique kind of torture. My mentor, Mike is a prime example, he owns three franchises and for ten years, his biggest professional stresses have revolved around trying to exit them. If my successful mentor struggles to escape a bad franchise, please understand the risks involved.

If you are unwilling to put in the work required to buy an independent, cash-flowing business, your best alternative is to simply put your $50,000 into an S&P 500 index fund and let it sit for twenty years.

If you're ready to do the work, keep reading.

Chapter 4 | The Panic Attack (Know Who You Are)

It was 2021, and I was thirty-six years old. By this time, I had achieved my fourth business exit, grown tremendously in my faith, and had been working hard to try and live my life as Jesus did.

Well, needless to say, I am a Christian, not a saint. Even through my acknowledgment of my own brokenness, there were still pitfalls waiting for me.

My wife, our kids, and our best friends, the Bennetts, went to visit a good mutual friend in College Station. It was a great evening. The kids got to play endlessly, and the grown-ups got to enjoy hanging out with one another like "old times." To paint the picture, "old times" meant having more drinks than you should, playing board games, and staying up way too late.

The evening passed with a lot of enjoyment, but the morning came quickly. I was one of the first to wake up and went out to get donuts and kolaches for everyone. However, I had to admit I was not feeling great. Surprisingly, I felt much worse than expected.

I started to overthink why I felt worse. Was I feeling worse because of the COVID vaccine shot I had taken three weeks prior which I was on the fence for? Was I having a delayed reaction? Nevertheless, I decided to ignore it. After a couple of hours hanging out, we packed up to make the drive home from College Station. I asked my wife to drive since I wasn't 100%.

When we stopped to use the restroom at a gas station, I jumped out of the car and puked in the bushes. (Seriously, what is it with me and puking at gas stations?). My wife was wondering why everyone was looking at us, and then she noticed the state I was in.

We got back on the road, but as we were driving, I started to feel worse and genuinely began thinking I was having a severe adverse medical reaction to something. FYI, I am a person who never goes to the doctor or the ER unless there is a bone visibly protruding from my skin—and even then, I might hesitate—but I turned to my wife and asked her to call an ambulance.

Mind you, we were in the middle of nowhere. While she was discussing with the operator where we should go, we drove by the Milan Volunteer Fire Department. I told her to pull over. I knew most firefighters have medical training, and if someone was there, they could at least perform CPR if I went down. By this time, I was confident my arm was tingling and I may be on a verge of a heart attack.

As it happened, one firefighter was there setting up for a charity event they were having that week. We parked, and while my wife was still on the phone with dispatch, I got out of the car to speak with him. I almost didn't make it. It felt as if three people jumped on my back as I was walking. Each step was slower and slower as I felt my body completely crashing.

I eventually collapsed onto a bench, and the firefighter came over to evaluate me. He took my vitals, noted that everything looked completely normal, and then asked me calmly, "Do you ever have panic attacks?"

I chuckled. Immediately, without a single second of hesitation, I scoffed, ***"No. I am not weak."***

Well, sitting there waiting for the ambulance to arrive, being reassured that my heart rate and vitals were perfectly fine, I started to question myself. *Am I having a panic attack? Am I overreacting and totally in my own head? I can't be weak... but is this a panic attack?*

The ambulance arrived, hooked me up to the EKG, ran their tests, and asked me the exact same question: "Do you have panic attacks?"

By this time—about thirty minutes from the initial phone call—I felt fine. Almost like nothing had ever happened. That crushing, barely-walking feeling was entirely gone.

Sure enough, I had experienced a panic attack. And sure enough, I was "weak". God has a beautiful, highly effective way of humbling you sometimes, and looking back, I am so grateful for it.

I share this story because, at the time, I knew I was broken, but my ego still blinded me to my own deficiencies. I encourage you to deeply self-reflect—preferably without needing a panic attack to do it—and identify exactly what deficiencies you may have when it comes to your acquisition endeavor. What is your real experience? What are your actual blind spots?

Knowing your true strengths and weaknesses will dictate how you prepare and ultimately succeed. Do not be an arrogant, thirty-six-year-old me.

In my years of selling businesses, I have worked with thousands of buyers, and I have found that they almost always fall into three distinct groups. Do any of the below resonate with you? If so, using the knowledge to identify which group you share similarities to is the first step in dropping your ego and fixing your strategy.

1. The Corporate Buyer

This buyer has spent years in Corporate America. They climbed the ladder, worked hard, and did everything society said they should do: they went to college, got a degree, found a great job, advanced, and perhaps got laid off once or twice.

Eventually, they realize they are working 40 to 60 hours a week building an empire for someone else. They have an "aha" moment and realize they could be doing it for themselves. They usually have a solid 401(k) to fund the acquisition, or they've managed to save a few hundred thousand dollars in cash. They are highly capable, but they must learn to adapt their sluggish corporate mindset to the fast-paced, messy realities of small business.

The Corporate Buyer is usually the most likely to succeed at acquiring a business, assuming they don't hire bad advisors. They tend to view things factually and are willing to accept sound advice. The only issue they tend to face is not knowing the best strategy for finding a high-quality company. This lack of deal flow often leads to desperation, causing them to settle and buy a company they shouldn't. *Don't do that!*

> 👁 **Note From The Lender's Desk**
>
> *On the banking side, we genuinely like the Corporate Buyer. They bring structured management skills, financial literacy, and professional accountability to the table. However, they almost always start their search at the wrong end of what I call the* ***Possible–Probable Spectrum****.*
>
> *Initially, corporate buyers hunt exclusively for deals on the Possible end of the spectrum—meaning they chase textbook-perfect, flawless companies that don't actually exist on Main Street. But after a few rounds of hitting reality walls, they quickly adjust, drop the corporate rigidness, and learn to seek out Probable caliber deals—real-world, slightly messy, highly profitable operations that a bank can actually finance.*
>
> *With just a bit of coaching and adaptability, this becomes a highly capable, top-tier buyer. Because of their background, they are often far more self-aware and open to hearing about their operational blind spots than a typical ego-driven buyer. If you can check your corporate bureaucracy at the door and remain coachable, lenders will actively fight to fund your deal.*

2. The "Wanna-Be" Private Equity (PE) Buyer

I will apologize ahead of time if you fall into this bucket. As a follower of Christ, I probably need to reevaluate what is in my heart, because I must admit: this type of buyer annoys me tremendously, and the initial thoughts that go through my head when I deal with them are not always godly.

The core issue is that they start the relationship with a lie. They present themselves to brokers and sellers in a way that is fundamentally deceptive. When you're an individual or two partners, who have never raised money or don't have a ready fund of capital and never will, presenting as a PE is misleading and unnecessary. It is like me telling you I am a towering 6-foot-tall man, when a quick glance at a photo proves I am only 5'8" (ugh... okay, fine, I'm 5'7").

I've found that the PE Buyer can be the most frustrating buyer to work with. These buyers are usually highly book-smart, but their confidence drastically exceeds their real-world small business experience. You will find them asking deep due diligence type questions at the wrong stages of the transaction, focus too heavily into spreadsheets, lean on bad advisors, and make unreasonable offers.

They are incredibly easy to identify, and they are a dime a dozen:

- They create an LLC and present themselves as a massive firm, inserting terms like "Venture," "Capital," or "Partners" into their name.
- They create a sleek website with absolutely no real substance—just a bio and their "acquisition criteria."
- They claim to have an endless supply of investors backing them. In reality, they usually only have a fraction of the down payment. Those investors say they will back the buyer, but when push comes to shove and it is time to wire the funds, the money rarely materializes.
- They are endlessly searching for a unicorn: *$500,000 to $2,000,000 EBITDA, recurring revenue, an absentee retiring owner, and absolutely zero to minimal risk* (seriously, what are you thinking? If that comes across my desk, I am buying it).
- They have consumed way too much textbook or online content from influencers promising perfect deals.

If you find yourself in this category, all hope is not lost. You are likely way smarter and harder-working than I am. We just need to point you in the right direction. If you can put your pride aside and take a position of genuine learning, the sky is the limit for you. But if you refuse to adapt, you will overcomplicate transactions and struggle to ever find true success acquiring or running a business.

👁 Note From The Lender's Desk: Operators vs. Spreadsheet Jockeys

These are often the buyers I see spending a bit too much time looking for the perfect scenario on the "Possible" side of the spectrum and spreadsheets. They are almost always incredibly smart, strong, and highly capable buyers, but that real-world capability can easily be overlooked when a deal is viewed strictly through a financial model/spreadsheet.

At the end of the day, banks look to finance business operators, not just spreadsheet operators. *While having a pristine, hyper-optimized spreadsheet is a fantastic asset, numbers alone can't steer a company through day-to-day realities like material cost spikes or staff transitions.*

When you pitch a deal to a bank, make sure you can confidently answer one core question: "Why this specific business, and why you?" If you can answer that with passion and clarity without leaning entirely on your cash flow projections or DSCR metrics, you prove to the bank that you aren't just analyzing an asset—you are ready to lead it.

🔑 Secret from the Broker's Desk

If a business generating $500,000 to $2,000,000 in EBITDA, with recurring revenue, an absentee owner, and low risk in a good industry actually comes across my desk, I am buying it myself. You are crazy to think otherwise.

3. The "Rooting For You" Buyer

This group of buyers is a massive part of what inspired me to write this book. I relate to them deeply. I find these buyers inspiring because they are desperately trying to provide a better future for their loved ones, yet they are the most likely to fall victim to the social media money grabs teaching them how to "Get Rich Buying a Business."

This group comes in many forms. It could be a single mother trying to build a better future for her family, a father wanting more for his children, or a person who had a rough upbringing and is actively rewriting their story. In many cases, they did life backwards, just like I did.

When I was in high school, I was pretty smart. My mom told me that if I got straight A's, I could do whatever I wanted. So, during my freshman and sophomore years, I got straight A's and qualified for "Running Start," a dual-credit college program. But I was a teenager with absolutely no guidance. I used my freedom to party, and I ultimately dropped out of high school in my junior year. Later, I enrolled in a completion program at that same college and finished a year and a half of classes in three months just to technically graduate on time.

I always joke that I am the smartest dumb person I know. I never went back to college and never received a formal degree. This caused me to be overlooked for countless job opportunities, leading me down a path where my only options were to accept a low-income job selling gutters during a drought, or take a massive risk to become an entrepreneur. (Thank you again, Tara, for encouraging me to take the risk; it changed the trajectory of our lives forever).

Statistically, the "Rooting For You" buyer is the least likely to succeed at acquiring a business. I am not saying they won't succeed in running one—they have the grit for it—but they lack the fundamental experience, the liquid resources, or the network of friends who can point them in the right direction during the search phase.

They get easily discouraged because they are completely unaware of the brutal challenges they face. An online influencer sold them a dream and made it appear easy. After a few months of hitting brick walls, they give up and accept the status quo.

I want to change that.

Understanding your strengths, your weaknesses, and your blind spots is the key to being successful. Check your ego at the door.

Chapter 5 | Get Educated (Ignorance is Expensive)

In 2011, my first daughter was born. I was in a very new relationship with my wife, Tara; we were not yet married, and we were trying to figure life out—or rather, I was desperately trying to figure life out.

I was quickly learning that making $45,000 a year selling gutters was a great wage for a single, twenty-five-year-old guy who shared an apartment and only needed beer money. But to raise a family in the manner I wanted, it wasn't even close to enough. Like any loving parent, I wanted my daughter to have a solid foundation. I didn't want her to experience life the way I did: poor, unstable, and lacking rooted values.

Even with the burning desire to provide more for my daughter, I was completely lost. Four months later, I was running out of money. I wasn't sure how I was going to pay the next month's rent, buy food, or support my new family.

By God's grace, Tara had inherited the remaining balance of her Texas Tomorrow College fund—about $9,000. Because we were still figuring out our relationship, we hadn't discussed finances deeply. When I finally swallowed my pride and came to her with my dilemma, she revealed that we had a little more runway than I thought. More importantly, she pushed me to consider starting my own business.

Tara wisely pointed out that selling gutters in Texas during a drought was not exactly the most lucrative career path. I was in the wrong industry. Instead of trying to catch water that wasn't falling, she told me I should start providing it.

That advice took me back to 2006, when I first moved to Texas and lived with my brother. He had a neighbor with the nicest home in a beautiful community, a massive RV, an immaculate lawn, and a nanny who drove a Hummer. He was just a normal, everyday guy—nothing special. He had achieved all of this simply by owning an irrigation company.

I figured if he could do it, why couldn't I?

I started looking into it. It turned out that becoming a Licensed Irrigator at the time only required a one-week class and a state test. Furthermore, I noticed that absolutely no one in the local industry was focusing on Search Engine Optimization (SEO), building a quality website, or gathering Google reviews. So, I got my license, built a strategy, and started my first business: Austex Sprinklers.

It was a success right out of the gate... well, except for the part where I had to hire my brother's neighbor, a plumber named Wes, to come bail me out at my very first appointment. (Thanks, Wes).

But despite my rookie mistakes, the business took off for two distinct reasons:

1. A Sound Strategy for Customer Acquisition

This is crucial whether you are starting a business from scratch or buying an existing one. I focused heavily on my digital presence when my competitors weren't. Today, when I look at a business to buy, the absolute first thing I examine is how they find their customers. Do they have hundreds of five-star reviews and a predictable marketing engine, or do they rely entirely on word-of-mouth and a twenty-year-old Rolodex? Depending on the answer, I will or will not buy a business based on this point alone. Understanding Customer Acquisition and having a fool-proof plan is a must. You can't succeed if no one pays for the service.

👁 Note From The Lender's Desk: The Value of a Growth Angle

Lenders don't always need you to be a master technician; we need to know you can lead a team and grow the top line.

The very first business acquisition I ever closed with Alex, the buyer had absolutely zero technical experience in that specific industry sector, but his elevator pitch to our underwriting department was ironclad. He told us: "The business currently relies on billing insurance but is only onboarded with three primary carriers. I come from the insurance space, and I have deep personal relationships at seven other major carriers who will fast-track my onboarding process. That alone will instantly expand our territory and drive massive new revenue."

It was a brilliant, highly realistic growth strategy that provided an operational edge even the current seller didn't have and couldn't replicate. Because that buyer brought a concrete customer acquisition playbook to the table, our credit risk department was completely comfortable moving past his lack of direct industry experience and funding the loan. If you show a lender how you are going to protect and scale the revenue engine, the bank will stand right behind you.

2. Setting Expectations

Through my personal experience—and from observing the many successful companies I've sold since—I've learned that the common denominator of success is setting expectations correctly for both customers and employees. We are not perfect, but we can communicate. If you make a mistake, own it immediately. If you come from a genuine place, people will forgive you. What pisses people off is when a contractor says they will be there at 2:00 PM on a Wednesday and completely ghosts them. If you are running late, call the customer before they leave work early to meet you.

Because I followed those two rules, the business grew faster than I could comprehend. By 2014—the year I ended up taking a nap at a Murphy's Gas Station—I had a highly successful, cash-flowing company. In hindsight, I probably never should have sold it, but I did it for one simple reason: I didn't understand business.

Despite the money I was making, I always felt like my company was a fragile house of cards that could collapse at any moment. When I went through the sales process, I didn't know what a balance sheet was, I didn't know how to value a company, and I had no idea what a proper Profit & Loss statement should look like. If I had been more knowledgeable, I would have had 10x more success with my first business and likely walked away with significantly more money.

Don't be ignorant like I was. Ignorance is expensive.

Luckily, my next venture—a company called Rainboxx, where I co-invented a wire-free acoustic irrigation valve—led me to five incredible advisors. These were highly successful, retired CEOs who took me under their wing. They taught me how to think like a successful executive and how to operate like a true entrepreneur.

Without their teachings and mentorship, I wouldn't have achieved the success I have today. To be clear, Rainboxx eventually failed. But what I learned from those men was far more valuable than the time and money I lost.

My goal is for this book to be the exact same type of blessing I received from those grumpy old men who met with me for a couple of hours every week for two years. I truly hope it enables you to find a great business, acquire it safely, and secure your own financial freedom.

Let's get to business.

Chapter 6 | No B.S. Guide To Buying A Business

You have survived the reality checks. You know how to filter through the BS. You know the challenge you face when it comes to buying a business.

Now, we move from theory to action.

What follows is the exact, step-by-step playbook you need to confidently acquire a business. Do not skip steps. Do not try to outsmart the process. If you follow this guide with discipline and speed, you will separate yourself from 99% of the buyers in the market.

Let's get to work.

Step 1: Learn The Language

The Terminology of a Deal

Master these terms immediately. They are the foundational language of every transaction and will dictate the next several months of your acquisition process.

- **Profit and Loss Statement (P&L):** A snapshot of the company's financial performance (revenue and expenses) over a specific period of time, like a year or a month.
- **Balance Sheet:** A snapshot of the company's financial health at a single moment in time. It shows the business's Assets, Liabilities, and Equity.
- **Asset List:** An inventory of all physical and intangible assets included in the sale. For example: cars, machinery, domains, social media accounts, trademarks, and computers.
- **Liabilities:** What the company owes. This includes accounts payable, outstanding loans, mortgages, and accrued expenses. In a standard Asset Sale, the buyer typically does not assume the seller's liabilities.

- **Letter of Intent (LOI):** A non-binding agreement presented by a Buyer to a Seller. It states: "If everything presented is true and accurate, here is what I am willing to pay, and here are my major deal terms."
- **Definitive Agreement:** The final, legally binding contract that consummates the transaction. This typically takes the form of an Asset Purchase Agreement (APA) or Equity Purchase Agreement (EPA).
- **SBA 7(a) Loan:** A bank loan insured by the Small Business Administration. It is the most common loan for acquiring businesses under $5,000,000, allowing Buyers to purchase a business with as little as 5% to 10% down.
- **Debt Service:** The cash required over a given period to cover the repayment of interest and principal on your acquisition loan. If your business doesn't generate enough cash to cover the Debt Service, the business fails.
- **Working Capital:** The operating liquidity available to a business for its day-to-day operations. It is the cash baseline required to fund inventory, make payroll, and cover immediate overhead before your customers' accounts receivable actually clear and hit your bank account.
- **CapEx (Capital Expenditures):** The funds used by a company to acquire, upgrade, and maintain physical assets such as vehicles, machinery, facilities, technology, or specialized equipment. CapEx represents the long-term investments required to keep the business operationally sound and competitive.
- **Seller Financing:** A structure where the seller acts as the bank, allowing you to pay a portion of the purchase price directly to them over time with interest. This keeps the seller financially invested in your post-sale success.

👁 **Note From The Lender's Desk**

Let's address a massive marketing gimmick you are going to see on almost every single listing: the words "SBA Pre-Qualified" or "SBA Pre-Approved" slapped all over the a for sale listing or on the front page of a Broker's Confidential Information Memorandum (CIM).

As a veteran lender, let me tell you how the marketing magic is created. A broker will frequently email a bank a glossy marketing flyer (the CIM) and ask us for a term sheet or a pre-qualification letter based purely on their own written narrative. Now, a professional broker should include the last three years of corporate tax returns and current Year-To-Date financials alongside that request—but a shocking number of them do not.

That means a bank lender often hands out an "SBA pre-qualified" stamp based entirely on blind faith and unverified marketing claims. There are loads of brokers in this industry whose beautifully presented Seller's Discretionary Earnings (SDE) calculations inside the CIM are completely fictional and are simply not reflected anywhere on the actual business tax returns.

Never assume a listing is safe just because a flyer says a bank looked at it. Always force your lender to cross-reference the hard tax data before you believe a word of the marketing packet.

- **Indemnification:** A legal clause where one party agrees to compensate the other for certain damages or losses. For example, the Seller indemnifies you against any undisclosed lawsuits or tax liens that occurred prior to closing.
- **Hold Backs:** A portion of the purchase price held in a third-party escrow account after closing to ensure the seller fulfills specific post-closing obligations, or to cover potential indemnification claims.
- **LLC (Limited Liability Company):** A common corporate structure that protects owners from personal responsibility for the company's debts or liabilities.

- **C-Corp:** A legal structure for a corporation in which the owners (shareholders) are taxed separately from the entity.
- **Confidential Information Memorandum (CIM):** The detailed prospectus created by the broker. You receive this after signing a Non-Disclosure Agreement (NDA). It details the business's operations, financials, and selling points.

How to Value a Business

Understanding how businesses are valued is critical. The most commonly accepted metric for sub-$5M businesses is the Income Approach (i.e., valuing the business based on what the current ownership earns).

To execute this, calculate the business's Seller's Discretionary Earnings (SDE) and multiply it by an adjusted multiple based on industry type, comparable sales, and associated risk.

To begin the valuation process, request the following documents:

- Last Three Years of Tax Returns
- Last Three Years of Profit and Loss Statements (Ideally in a monthly Excel format)
- Current Year-To-Date (YTD) Profit and Loss Statements
- Last Three Years of Balance Sheets
- Current YTD Balance Sheet
- Current Asset List of items valued at $250 or more
- Current Inventory Cost and Average Cost

Important Note: Most Sellers will withhold highly sensitive information (like tax returns) until further in the acquisition process.

Seller's Discretionary Earnings (SDE)

To calculate the valuation, first determine the SDE (sometimes called "Owner's Free Cash Flow").

SDE = Net Ordinary Income + Non-Essential Expenses (Positive Add-Backs) - Essential Expenses Not Captured (Negative Add-Backs)

- **Positive Add-Backs:** If the business pays for the current owner's health insurance, life insurance, cell phone bill, personal vehicle, vacations, or personal utilities, add these back to the bottom line. They are discretionary and won't be an expense for you as the new owner. Also add back Depreciation, Amortization, and one-time business expenses (like a $40,000 website update that occurs once a decade).
- **Negative Add-Backs (The Trap):** Identify any new expenses you will incur that the current owner does not. For example, if the owner owns the real estate and operates rent-free, you must deduct the new commercial lease expense you will incur. Another common negative add-back is the cost to hire a new employee to replace an owner's spouse who currently works for free.

Factor in all positive and negative add-backs, then total them to determine the true SDE.

> ⚠ **Mentor's Warning**
>
> *Scrutinize businesses with massive add-backs. Ensure all add-backs are legitimate and substantiate them entirely during due diligence.*

> 👁 **Note From The Lender's Desk: The Add-Back Reality Check for SBA Loan Calculations**
>
> *When you are looking at an SDE recast, remember that what a broker writes into a marketing package isn't always what a bank's credit department will actually allow. Lenders look at add-backs under a microscope, and there are two major traps you need to watch out for.*
>
> *First, do not automatically assume the bank will accept every discretionary "owner perk" listed in the CIM. A lender is highly unlikely to approve adding back items like*

personal utilities, cell phone bills, family vacations, or general vehicle expenses—unless they are explicitly provable, business-essential costs like a verified commercial vehicle lease expense and associated auto insurance.

Second, and most importantly: ***Owner's Distributions are absolutely NOT add-backs.*** *This is a fundamental accounting rule that even trained business brokers with a long string of letters after their names frequently miss. Owner's distributions are Balance Sheet items, not Income Statement items. Because of that, there is no actual "Owner's Distribution expense" reducing Net Income that you can magically add back.*

Brokers usually make this mistake because they look at an unreconciled General Ledger (GL) when preparing their initial financial recast. At that exact moment, the distribution might look like a regular line-item expense on the GL. But the second the accountant or bookkeeper performs a formal reconciliation, that distribution moves right where it legally belongs: onto the Balance Sheet. If an SDE calculation looks artificially inflated because a broker tried to add back distributions, the bank will halt the deal. Trust the reconciled tax returns, not an unverified ledger.

The Multiple

Next, determine the multiple. Most Main Street businesses sell for a multiple of 1x to 4x their SDE. Businesses in this bracket rarely command a multiple above 4x because the loan's debt payments would render the acquisition mathematically impossible for a Buyer.

Industry type and SDE volume primarily dictate the multiple. A highly desirable industry increases demand, and a higher SDE makes the business safer and more desirable.

Use this reliable baseline breakdown:

- **$0 – $100,000 SDE:** 1x (or not sellable)
- **$100,001 – $150,000 SDE:** 1x to 2x

- **$151,001 – $200,000 SDE:** 2x to 2.5x
- **$201,001 – $300,000 SDE:** 2.5x to 3x
- **$300,001 – $400,000 SDE:** 3x to 3.5x
- **$400,001 – $500,000 SDE:** 3.25x to 4x
- **$500,000+ SDE:** 4x

After determining your starting multiple based on the SDE size, adjust it based on Risk. High risk lowers the multiple; low risk raises it.

Factors that increase risk (and decrease value) include:

- **Financial History:** Declining year-over-year sales.
- **Customer Concentration:** One or two clients generating a massive share of total revenue.
- **Key Man Risk:** The owner is the business. If they leave, the core value leaves with them.
- **Industry Concerns:** Heavy regulatory licensing, high-liability models, or declining sectors.
- **Staffing Concerns:** The owner works 70 hours a week, or the staff consists entirely of family members who will exit after the sale.

Risk Adjustment Examples

Opportunity 1 (High Risk): SDE is $500,000. The owner holds the primary specialty license, quotes all bids, and directly manages contractors.

> Starting Multiple: 4x (based on high SDE)
>
> Adjusted Multiple: 2x
>
> Reason: Massive Key Man Risk. Without the owner, operations paralyze.

Opportunity 2 (Low Risk): SDE is $200,000. The owner works 20-25 hours a week handling payroll. A loyal staff of 5 handles all day-to-day operations. The owner is selling to have a baby.

> Starting Multiple: 2.25x

Adjusted Multiple: 3x

Reason: The staff de-risks dependency on the owner, and the seller has a highly verifiable, logical reason for selling.

Opportunity 3 (The Gold Standard): SDE is $600,000. 25 years in business. The owner works 40 hours a week. They employ a tenured team of 13, and the owner will stay for a one-year transition.

Starting Multiple: 4x

Adjusted Multiple: 4x

Reason: The 25-year history, strong team, and extensive transition period offer massive buyer confidence. (Note: You still need relevant skills to replace this owner's day to day role in the business, but it remains a premium asset).

Multiply your SDE by your Adjusted Multiple to establish your initial valuation.

The Hidden Variables

Before you jump to a conclusion on any deal's math, you must account for three silent, deal-altering elements: **Inventory**, **Working Capital**, and **CapEx (Capital Expenditures)**.

When a broker lists a business for a specific purchase price, that number is almost never the *final* amount of cash you need to close or survive the first year.

- **The Inventory Bump:** Most Main Street transactions are structured as asset sales where the price is stated as "$1,500,000 *plus inventory at cost*." If that business carries **$150,000** worth of inventory on the shelves, your actual purchase price just skyrocketed to $1,650,000. Because the total transaction size went up, your bank-mandated 10% down payment just increased by **$15,000** out of your personal pocket.

- **The Working Capital Drain:** On day one of taking over, you have to pay employees, keep the lights on, and buy raw materials before a single customer invoice clears and turns into cash. If the business requires **$100,000** in working capital to operate safely, you either have to inject an extra $100,000 of your own liquid cash at the closing table, or roll it into the bank loan. If you roll it in, your total loan size increases, your monthly debt service payments go up, and the cash flow you expected to take home as personal earnings drops.

- **The CapEx Time Bomb:** Capital Expenditures are the long-term investments required to keep the business physically functioning—like replacing a delivery truck, upgrading a software stack, or putting a new roof on the facility. If you look at the company's asset list and see machinery held together by duct tape and prayer, you are staring at a massive CapEx liability. If you have to spend **$50,000** in Year 2 to replace a failing piece of equipment, that cash comes directly out of your bottom-line profits. Alternatively, if the bank notices this risk during underwriting, they may force a CapEx reserve holdback at closing, meaning you have to bring even more cash to the table up front.

Never analyze a deal based purely on the base purchase price. These operating and capital requirements heavily affect your total cash layout. If you don't bake them into your calculations early, you will either get hit with a devastating cash shortage at the closing table, or realize too late that your net, real-world earnings are significantly lower than what you modeled on your spreadsheet.

👁 **Note From The Lender's Desk: The Day-One Liquidity Trap**

One of the most common ways buyers fail is by going completely "all-in" on their initial equity injection just to satisfy the bank's down payment requirement, without budgeting a single cent for immediate operational cash flow. If the business needs baseline working capital to function or future CapEx and you haven't structurally accounted for it ahead of time, the chances of your new acquisition failing escalate dramatically.

The Ultimate BS Filter: The Test of Reasonableness

The asking price presented by a Seller rarely reflects an accurate valuation. Calculate your own valuation and apply basic logic to ensure the deal supports your livelihood.

Use the "Test of Reasonableness." This calculation views the acquisition strictly from the Buyer's perspective and clearly demonstrates to a Seller why their asking price may be out of touch with reality.

To run the test, take the asking price and assume you are financing it through a standard SBA 7(a) loan. Assume a 10% down payment, a 120-month term (10 years), and an interest rate around Prime + 2% (use 10% for easy math).

Calculate your yearly debt service, then subtract that debt service from the Owner's SDE. The remaining number is your actual free cash flow..

- **The Failed Test:** A business is listed for $500,000, but the current SDE is only $100,000. You put down $50,000 (10%) and finance the remaining $450,000. Your loan payment is approximately $5,700 a month, or $68,400 a year. If you buy this business, your take-home pay is only $31,600 a year. This fails the test. You can earn double that managing a restaurant without risking a $50,000 down payment.
- **The Passed Test:** The Seller reduces the price to $185,000. Your debt service drops to roughly $25,200 yearly. As the new owner, your expected take-home pay is $74,800 a year. Does this pass the test? If the

business requires 15 hours a week of your time, yes. If it requires 50 hours of grueling labor, no.

Here are three simplified Test of Reasonableness calculations across different business sizes:

Example Business 1 (Large Target)

Seller's SDE: $515,000

Metric	Example 1	Example 2	Example 3
Sales Price	$1,990,000	$1,749,000	$1,490,000
10% Down Payment / Equity Injection	$200,000	$175,000	$150,000
Typical Capitalized Financing Expenses (approx. 2% of the loan amount)	$40,000	$35,000	$30,000
Total Financed Loan Amount	$1,750,000	$1,539,000	$1,310,000
Yearly Debt Payments (10yr @ 10%)	$266,016 ($22,168/mo)	$233,940 ($19,495/mo)	$199,128 ($16,594/mo)
New Owner's Estimated Yearly Income (Assuming a $515,000 SDE Average)	$248,984	$281,060	$315,872

Example Business 2 (Medium Target)

Seller's SDE: $406,000

Metric	Example 1	Example 2	Example 3
Sales Price	$1,299,000	$1,199,000	$990,000
10% Down Payment / Equity Injection	$130,000	$120,000	$100,000
Total Financed Loan Amount	$1,169,000	$1,079,000	$890,000
Yearly Debt Payments (10yr @ 10%)	$185,376 ($15,448/mo)	$171,108 ($14,259/mo)	$142,560 ($11,880/mo)
New Owner's Estimated Yearly Income (Assuming a $420,000 SDE Average)	$234,624	$248,892	$277,440
New Owner's Estimated Yearly Income (Assuming a $406,000 SDE)	$220,624	$234,892	$263,440

Example Business 3 (Small Target)

<u>Seller's SDE: $105,000</u>

Metric	Example 1	Example 2	Example 3
Sales Price	$299,000	$199,000	$149,000
10% Down Payment / Equity Injection	$30,000	$20,000	$15,000
Total Financed Loan Amount	$269,000	$179,000	$134,000
Yearly Debt Payments (10yr @ 10%)	$42,648 ($3,554/mo)	$28,380 ($2,365/mo)	$21,240 ($1,770/mo)
New Owner's Estimated Yearly Income (Assuming a $105,000 SDE Average)	$62,352	$76,620	$83,760

Note From The Lender's Desk

- *Never assume a listing is safe just because a flyer says "Pre-Approved" or "Pre-Qualified". Many Banks give out "SBA Pre-Qualified" or "SBA Pre-Approved" stamps based entirely on blind faith and unverified financials. Always force your lender to cross-reference the hard tax data before you believe a word of the marketing.*

👁 Note From The Lender's Desk: The 60-Second "Max Financing" Napkin Math

Max financing does not indicate business value. *You can agree to pay a seller a ridiculous, overinflated valuation, but the bank is only ever going to finance the actual cash-flow capacity of the business. That cap is your max financing baseline.*

When a broker sends me a new CIM, I don't waste time building out a massive, multi-tab deal spreadsheet right away. Instead, I open the basic calculator app on my phone and run a quick filtering calculation to see if the deal is even worth my time.

You can use this exact same underwriting shortcut:

1. *Start with the stated SDE.*
2. *Subtract a **Realistic Living Expense (RLE)**—the absolute minimum cash salary you need to pull out of the business to pay your personal mortgage, buying power, and groceries.*
3. *Divide that remaining number by **1.5**. This instantly gives you the maximum annual debt service the business can support while maintaining a safe **1.5x Debt Service Coverage Ratio (DSCR)**.*

Max Annual Debt Service = SDE - Realistic Living Expenses / 1.5

*Let's look at a real-world example. Say you get a CIM pitching an SDE of **$500,000**.*

- ***Step 1:** Start with **$500,000** SDE.*
- ***Step 2:** Subtract your personal living expenses (let's call it **$100,000**). You are left with **$400,000** of cash flow available before debt service.*
- ***Step 3:** Divide **$400,000** by **1.5**. Your maximum allowable annual debt service is **~$266,000**.*

*Now, open any free loan calculator on your phone. Plug in a standard **10-year term** and a conservative **9.75% interest rate** (which reflects WSJ Prime + 3.00%). With just a tiny bit of quick trial-and-error adjustments to the loan principal, you will find that a **~$1,700,000** loan amount gives you an annual debt payment of exactly **$266,000**.*

*Boom. You're done. Your maximum bank loan is **$1.7 million**. You must build your entire offer, equity injection, and seller note structure around that baseline number. If the broker is demanding a **$3 million** purchase price on that **$500,000** SDE, you instantly know the math is completely broken from a lenders standpoint without killing a single extra brain cell on deep diligence.*

Step 2: Define Your Target Business (The Wide Net & Guardrails)

Operating with too singular of a focus guarantees you will never buy a business. Holding out for a hyper-specific unicorn—like a plumbing company doing exactly $1.5M in a specific five-mile zip code with an absentee owner—will leave you searching for a decade.

Cast a wide net and remain flexible to different industries. However, recognize the massive difference between a wide net and a sloppy net.

A sloppy buyer reviews businesses listed for sale without knowing their capital limits, risk tolerance, or operational skill set. A smart buyer casts a wide net but establishes strict parameters before inquiring on a listed business.

To define your target business, build your guardrails by determining four key metrics: liquid capital for the down payment,, buying power, risk tolerance, and operational skill set.

The Baseline: Your Down Payment

Your available down payment acts as the absolute bottleneck of your buying power. It is the single most critical factor in determining the size of the business you can acquire.

Your down payment must be liquid capital (cash on hand). This includes checking accounts, savings accounts, or easily liquidated brokerage accounts (stocks/ETFs).

Another highly effective down payment method is a 401(k) rollover (a ROBS strategy), allowing you to invest retirement funds into your newly formed company without triggering early withdrawal penalties. Options like personal lines of credit or HELOCs are occasionally permitted but face heavy bank scrutiny.

The most common vehicle for acquiring a business valued under $5,000,000 is an SBA 7(a) Loan. The traditional minimum down payment required for this loan type is 10%. Knowing this baseline dictates your maximum loan amount, **assuming the down payment is not 100% of your liquidity.**

Calculating Your Buying Power

Assume you plan to deploy a $50,000 down payment. Applying the standard 10% rule for an SBA 7(a) loan, that $50,000 down mathematically supports a $500,000 purchase price—provided that this $50,000 represents only a portion of your total net worth. As you will see in the lender's reality check below, banks look at your total liquidity pool, not just the down payment check

However, buying power is a range. Creative deal structures stretch your capital. With a willing Seller, you can leverage a "Stand-By Seller's Note" to reduce your required cash injection to 5%, effectively doubling your buying power to $1,000,000.

A buyer with $50,000 dedicated towards the down payment should primarily target businesses listed at $500,000, but can stretch up to $1,000,000 through negotiation. Targeting a business at the 5% equity mark requires a Seller Financing Note on full standby—meaning the Seller receives zero payments on that note until the bank loan clears.

Review this breakdown of maximum buying power based on standard and creative deal structures:

Available Down Payment	MAX Buying Power (Standard 10% Down)	MAX Buying Power (Creative 5% Down)
$10,000	$100,000	$200,000
$20,000	$200,000	$400,000
$30,000	$300,000	$600,000
$40,000	$400,000	$800,000
$50,000	$500,000	$1,000,000
$75,000	$750,000	$1,500,000
$100,000	$1,000,000	$2,000,000

Available Down Payment	MAX Buying Power (Standard 10% Down)	MAX Buying Power (Creative 5% Down)
$150,000	$1,500,000	$3,000,000
$200,000	$2,000,000	$4,000,000
$300,000	$3,000,000	$5,050,000 (SBA Loan Limits apply)
$500,000	$5,000,000	$5,250,000 (SBA Loan Limits apply)

Note From The Lender's Desk:

Banks never want to see a buyer go completely "all-in" and leave themselves with zero personal liquidity after a deal closes. So another way of determining buying potential is by total liquidity. A quick way to determine a safe business target size is to take the sum of a buyer's total verifiable liquid assets—which includes ***liquid cash, accessible 401(k)/IRA balances, and publicly traded stocks or bonds****—and multiply that total by* ***6.5x****.*

Realistic Max Loan Amount = Total Personal Liquidity x 6.5

Under this risk framework, a borrower with ***$100,000*** *in total liquid assets can realistically expect to qualify for roughly a* ***$650,000*** *bank loan unless creative deal structure workarounds are used. But remember: those structural workarounds are the exceptions, not the day-to-day underwriting rules.*

Risk Tolerance (Just Because You Can, Doesn't Mean You Should)

Once your buying power is established, objectively assess your risk tolerance.

Just because you can buy a $1,000,000 company doesn't mean you should. Acquiring a business requires taking on significant debt service. If the potential monthly payments exceed your comfort zone, lower your target value. Determine the absolute minimum yearly earnings you need to survive.

Calculate your net expected earnings after the bank gets paid.

The Math: You target a business listed for $500,000 with an SDE of $150,000. You put $50,000 down and finance $450,000. Under a standard 120-month term at a 10% interest rate, your yearly debt service is approximately $70,000.

Assuming no remaining cashflow is retained for growth or operation, your maximum take-home pay is $80,000 a year.

Does earning $80,000 a year justify taking on $450,000 in debt and risking a $50,000 down payment? For some, this buys freedom. For others, the debt stress outweighs the reward. Understand all risks: loan commitments, emergency reserves, and industry-specific liabilities.

The Mirror Test: Choosing Your Business Type

Determine your target industry by making three lists:

- **What are my skills?** Are you client-facing? Highly analytical? A strong operator? Aligning the business with your core competencies heavily mitigates the risk of failure. Ten years of construction management experience makes you a better fit for a roofing company than a software firm.
- **What do I like to do?** Do you prefer field work, or do you need to manage from a desk? Is your passion building teams? Answer these questions to ensure you do not buy yourself a high-paying prison sentence.
- **What do I hate to do?** If you hate working outside, avoid landscaping. If you despise corporate meetings, avoid B2B consulting. Defining your deal-breakers is just as important as defining your passions.

> ⚠ **Mentor's Warning - Why this business, why you?**
>
> *Buying a business that does not align with your operational skills—purely because the financials look attractive—is the fastest way to fail.A brilliant tech executive*

once bought a blue-collar hardscaping company based entirely on flawless spreadsheets. He hated waking up at 5:00 AM, hated the heat, and possessed zero ability to manage a crew of laborers. His corporate management skills did not translate, and he ran a highly profitable business into the ground.Respect the learning curve. Be brutally honest with yourself: Can I truly execute this operation? Do I actually want to work with these customers and employees every single day? If the answer is no, define a new target.

Step 3: Get Pre-Qualified

Do not begin scrolling through listings yet. Assemble your financial foundation first. **Preparation and speed dictate success in acquisitions.**

Finding a great business, waiting three days to think about it, and then spending two weeks waiting for a bank to pre-qualify you guarantees failure. A fully prepared buyer will lock up the deal while you are trading emails. Get the business under exclusivity as quickly as possible.

Prove You Belong at the Table

Getting pre-qualified establishes your true buying power, positions you to move instantly, and proves to Listing Brokers and Sellers that you are a legitimate buyer capable of closing.

> 🔑 **Secret from the Broker's Desk**
>
> *Not all banks are equal. Find a bank with dedicated, high-volume experience in business acquisitions. Avoid bankers who only underwrite one M&A deal a year.*

Execute these rules to secure the right lender and rate:

- **Use an SBA-Approved Lender:** This significantly expedites the process. Not every bank knows how to navigate the Small Business Administration's red tape. Secure a lender who processes these specific loans daily.
- **Ensure Industry-Agnostic Lending:** Large banks (like Chase or Wells Fargo) often harbor internal policies against lending to restaurants or construction companies. If your chosen bank restricts your target industry, it will kill the deal regardless of flawless financials.
- **Create a Bidding War (The Rule of Three):** Build relationships with at least three different lenders. When your offer is accepted, compare their term sheets to secure the best deal. This also protects you if one lender suddenly backs out of your specific industry.

- **The Responsiveness Test:** A slow banker suffocates a deal. Your banker should return calls within two hours 90% of the time. If they treat you like an afterthought during pre-qualification, they will paralyze the process during underwriting.

Experience Matters: Select a banker with multiple years of direct SBA loan experience to navigate the inevitable roadblocks that occur before closing.

👁 **A Note From The Lenders Desk**

How to Earn a Banker's Attention (and Avoid the Inbox Trash Can)

A productive lender's time is strictly guarded. If I receive a generic email from a searcher wanting to "grab 20 minutes to chat about next steps for pre-qualification," my response will always be a brief, automated email requesting three non-negotiables: an SBA Personal Financial Statement (PFS), a professional resume, and our bank's Personal Info Form. Turn those files around to me quickly, and then we will get a strategic call scheduled.

Similarly, if a buyer blindly drops a raw Confidential Information Memorandum (CIM) into my inbox with a lazy note asking, "Whaddya think about this business?"—I am not prioritizing your request and will respond accordingly. FYI, Lenders are not your free, outsourced due diligence screening service.

However, a buyer who has already taken the initiative to get pre-qualified ahead of time. When that prepared buyer emails me a live deal that falls into the realistic, "Probable" realm, accompanied by a draft LOI, corporate tax returns, and a completed M&A questionnaire, they get my attention immediately. Because they brought an actual transaction backed by real data, I can give them fast, high-impact initial feedback.

The Danger of "Turbo-Speed" Bankers

While you want an active, responsive banking partner, you must be incredibly wary of a lender who moves at an impossible pace without asking tough questions. A turbo speed banker who isn't deeply analyzing the file kills deals just as fast as a slow one.

It takes real time and focus for a commercial underwriter to evaluate a complex business relative to you as the unique operator, anticipate structural obstacles to closing, and brainstorm mitigants. A formal term sheet cranked out within a few hours of receiving a CIM should never be taken as a certainty to close.

More often than not, a lightning-fast term sheet simply means an aggressive lender is rushing to lock up your business and get your deal off the street before their competition does. They will wait to do the actual, painful math weeks later—frequently blowing up your transaction at the eleventh hour. Look for thoroughness, transparency, and a lender who asks the hard questions early.

Step 4: Line Up Counsel

Establish your legal shield before you need it. Secure a Business Attorney and set up the retainer immediately to save precious time once you find a promising business.

Note: Attorneys can kill deals. While legal protection is absolutely necessary, an arrogant attorney attempting to justify billable hours will blow up a highly profitable transaction. You need a pragmatic deal-maker.

Vet your Business Attorney using these guidelines:

- **Verify Their Specialty:** Ask directly if Business Transactions are their primary expertise. Many attorneys advertise M&A services but actually specialize in Family Law or Real Estate. A lack of focused M&A experience leads to higher bills and weaker protection.
- **Flashy Does Not Equal Competent:** High-profile firms often charge exorbitant rates without delivering superior results.

⚠ **Mentor's Warning**

A well-known law firm in Austin features two partners: one is excellent, the other is a deal-killer. The terrible partner over-lawyers every clause, fighting to the death over obscure indemnifications that have a 0.001% chance of occurring. This infuriates the Seller, stalls the process, and results in $50,000 legal bills for standard $800,000 transactions.Trust Your Gut: Interview multiple attorneys. If they talk down to you or act like they intend to "destroy" the seller's counsel, walk away. You are buying a business, not fighting a war. Hire a professional who protects your downside without losing sight of the finish line.

Note From The Lender's Desk

Let's be completely clear: as a bank, we absolutely want capable, sharp attorneys on our deals to protect our collateral and your investment. What I see far too often, however, are lawyers who are completely unfamiliar with small-to-medium business (SMB) lawyering.

Instead of moving the transaction forward, these corporate or generalist attorneys spend their billable hours making absolute mountains out of molehills, generally trying to demonstrate to everyone else in the transaction how smart they are. I have watched this exact behavior deeply frustrate both the buyer and the seller—and yes, sometimes it is the buyer's own counsel causing the head-banging frustration—until it completely scuttles a perfectly strong deal.

Never forget that the attorneys work for you, not the other way around. Ask for referrals to legal teams who are explicitly known and respected in the SMB world. If your SBA lender is active in business acquisitions, they will easily be able to hand you a list of pragmatic deal-makers who know how to protect your downside without killing the finish line.

Trust Your Gut: *Interview multiple attorneys. If they talk down to you or act like they intend to "destroy" the seller's counsel, walk away. You are buying a business, not fighting a war. Hire a professional who protects your downside without losing sight of the finish line.*

Step 5: Prepare A Template LOI

Maintain a professional, attorney-reviewed Letter of Intent (LOI) template on your computer, ready to customize instantly.

Instruct your attorney on the specific terms to include to prevent them from overcomplicating the document. Your mindset when submitting an LOI is straightforward: *"If everything presented is true and accurate, I am willing to acquire this business under these terms."* Verification happens later during Due Diligence.

Structure your LOI using these key deal terms:

Transaction Type: Asset vs. Equity

Specify an Asset or Equity sale. In an Asset sale, you acquire only the Assets of the business, protecting yourself from prior liabilities tied to the Seller's corporate entity (LLC/C-Corp). This is the preferred acquisition method.

An Equity Purchase (buying the actual entity) assumes higher risk but is occasionally necessary to transfer specific vendor contracts or grandfathered licenses. Default to an Asset Sale whenever possible.

Deal Structure: Allocation and Financing

Specify exactly how the purchase price will be allocated.

Seller Financing

Require at least 10% Seller Financing. This is standard in sub-$10,000,000 transactions and validates the following:

- The Seller believes the business will generate enough cash for you to repay the loan.
- The Seller believes you are capable of operating the business.
- The Seller is not hiding post-sale skeletons.

Important Note: Clearly explain why you require Seller Financing (e.g., to lower monthly debt obligations and maintain healthy working capital) rather than demanding it blindly.

Seller Financing on Stand-By

A "Full Stand-By" Seller Note means the Seller receives zero payments until your SBA Loan is paid off (typically Year 10). Sellers despise this structure, but it effectively cuts your required cash down payment in half.

To successfully pitch this, increase the overall purchase price. If a business is listed at $2,000,000 and you only have $150,000 down (below the standard 10%), offer $2,100,000. Request 10% Seller Financing split into two notes: a standard 5% note with immediate payments, and a 5% note on full standby.

- **The Buyer Benefit:** Down payment drops to $105,000, satisfying the bank's requirements while deferring massive acquisition costs.
- **The Seller Benefit:** Receives an above-asking-price offer upfront. The stand-by note becomes a no risk, high reward perk that may net them a $100K more down the road.

Inventory

Clearly state if inventory is included in the purchase price or calculated as an additional cost.

- **When Included:** Lowers your upfront cash requirements. You finance the inventory through the SBA loan, paying only the 5% or 10% down payment on its value. Ensure the LOI includes legal language requiring the Seller to leave "Normal Levels of Good, Salable Inventory associated with ordinary business operations."
- **When NOT Included (Plus Inventory):** Ensures you only pay for exactly what sits on the shelves at closing, forcing a hard count and allowing you to reject stagnant stock.

Conditions to Closing

List the explicit terms required to close. Examples include:

- All Assets transfer free and clear of any liens or liabilities.
- All necessary consents from third parties obtained.
- Contingent on Buyer securing necessary SBA funding.
- Contingent on successful lease transfer.
- Purchaser assumes no liabilities or obligations of Seller.
- Seller executes Non-Compete and Post Close Transition Agreement.

Due Diligence and Exclusivity Structure

Designate a structured period to conduct a comprehensive investigation and verify accuracy. This timeframe runs concurrently with Exclusivity.

Structure your due diligence and exclusivity as follows:

- **First 30 Days:** Included in the accepted LOI at no cost to the Buyer to verify the offering.
- **Extension 1 (30 Days):** Granted upon payment of a non-refundable $1,000 deposit applied to the purchase price.
- **Extension 2 (30 Days):** Granted upon proof of loan application deposit and accepted term sheet.
- **Extension 3 (30 Days):** Granted upon payment of a non-refundable $2,500 deposit applied to the purchase price.
- **Extension 4 (30 days):** Granted upon payment of a non-refundable $5,000 deposit applied to the purchase price.

This protects your position, prevents the Seller from entertaining other offers, and demonstrates your definitive financial commitment to closing the deal.

Request these standard Due Diligence items:

- Three years of Business Tax Returns
- Three years of Profit and Loss Statements (Monthly Excel format)
- Three years of Balance Sheets
- Monthly Bank Statements and Credit Card Statements

- Monthly Employee Detailed Payroll Reports
- Current Accounts Receivable / Payable
- All Active Agreements (Leases, Vendor Contracts)
- Detailed Asset List (Items over $250)
- Yearly Sales By Customer / Expenses By Vendor
- Company Formation Documents
- Insurance Policies and documentation of Past/Pending Lawsuits

Exclusivity/No Shop Clause

Bind the Seller to work only with you. This ensures you do not waste thousands of dollars on legal and accounting fees only to have the Seller accept a higher offer at the last minute. Allow mutual extensions of exclusivity if both parties agree.

Termination

Include clear termination guidelines to validate the Exclusivity clause:

- Automatically terminates if the Buyer does not extend exclusivity after the initial 30 days.
- Buyer may terminate anytime with written notice.
- Seller may terminate anytime only with written notice, a $5,000 penalty fee, and a full refund of all non-refundable deposits to the Buyer.

Confidentiality

Include a standard clause binding both parties to protect all shared confidential information.

Transition

Define the exact post-sale training required. Request at least 30 days of transition included in the purchase price. If a Seller rushes to exit without a valid health reason, treat it as a major red flag.

Example Transition Clause:

Transition Consulting: Seller agrees to assist Purchaser with the transition of operations, key accounts, and processes for up to 180 days:

- **Days 0–30:** Up to 20 hours/week of in-person, phone, or email support.
- **Days 31–180:** Up to 8 hours/week of phone or email support.
- **Days 31–365:** Purchaser may hire Seller at an agreed hourly rate for additional support.

Non-Compete

Require a Non-Compete clause. A Seller fighting aggressively to reduce this scope is a massive red flag. Establish a standard 3-to-5-year term with a geographically reasonable radius. (Overreaching, nationwide radiuses present poorly and stall negotiations.)

Target Closing Date

Manage expectations and formalize the timeline. Draft a schedule that includes the Loan Proposal Acceptance Date, First Draft of Definitive Agreement Date, Full Lending Approval, and Target Close Date.

Set the Target Closing Date as "120 days from execution of LOI or sooner."

Step 6: Prepare Proof of Funds

When inquiring about a business, proactively send redacted Proof of Funds covering at least 10% of the total asking price.

If the business is listed for $1,000,000, attach a document verifying $100,000 in liquid capital. Doing this upfront proves your financial capability to close the deal, elevating you from a tire-kicker to a top-tier prospect. Brokers review inquiries with attached Proof of Funds first.

Acceptable forms of proof include:

- Bank checking or savings statements
- Money market account statements
- Brokerage account statements (stocks/ETFs)
- 401(k) statements (if executing a ROBS strategy)

> ⚠ **Mentor's Warning**
>
> *Protect Yourself. Redact your account numbers, social security number, and highly sensitive data with a digital marker. The broker only needs your name, the date, the institution, and the available balance.*

Step 7: Prepare A Buyer Resume

Attach a one-page Buyer Resume alongside your Proof of Funds. This allows the broker to immediately verify your operational fit and easily pitch you to a protective Seller. Keep it concise.

Use this format for your initial inquiry:

> *Hi [Broker Name],*
>
> *I am pursuing this opportunity. My [Skillset/Industry] experience and [X] years in this field align perfectly with this operation. Attached is the signed NDA, Proof of Funds, and a one-page brief on my background.*
>
> *I look forward to reviewing the CIM.*
>
> *Kind Regards,*
>
> *[Your Name]*

This email confirms you possess the required funds, the relevant experience, and the professionalism to close a deal.

Step 8: Set Up Electronic Signing

Do not lose a deal over logistics. Expeditious action wins the match!

When a premium listing hits the market, sign the required NDA immediately. Waiting until you get back from vacation to print, physically sign, and scan a document wastes days. A prepared buyer signs electronically and receives the financials before you even find a pen.

Create an account with DocuSign, HelloSign, or Adobe Acrobat. Save your digital signature on your desktop and mobile device. Return documents within five minutes of receipt.

Your Acquisition Foundation is now complete.

Step 9: The Hunt (Sourcing and Screening Businesses)

With your capital, team, and introductory package prepared, you're ready to search.

The market for small businesses is fragmented. To find a highly profitable operation, work these three primary avenues:

- **The Public Markets/Websites (BizBuySell):** Set up daily alerts on BizBuySell and BusinessBroker.net. Because these platforms are crowded, deploy your polished introductory package immediately to cut through the noise. (Broker's Note: Utilize AI tools to comb these sites multiple times a day).
- **Direct Broker Relationships:** Build relationships to access "pocket listings" before they hit the public market. Sign up for "VIP Access" lists at top brokerages. Mail a physical resume and a $5 Starbucks gift card to top brokers to establish a direct connection. DON'T JUST EMAIL.
- **The Off-Market Approach:** Contact business owners directly via letters, LinkedIn, or cold calls. While 99% will ignore you, securing an exhausted owner who hasn't hired a broker allows you to negotiate with zero buyer competition.

The Golden Rule of the Hunt: Boring is Beautiful

Ignore the temptation to only look for "sexy" businesses.

Trendy coffee shops and boutique fitness studios are fun businesses to buy, however, profitable cash-flowing ones only come up ever so often. Boring B2B services, plumbing routes, and distribution companies generate the cash flow required to build actual wealth and are more frequently available.

Step 10: Initial Inquiry — The NDA

Brokers list businesses in a Confidential Manner (e.g., "Highly Profitable B2B Service Company in Travis County"). To access the financials, you must sign an NDA (Non-Disclosure Agreement).

Sign the NDA electronically and return it instantly with your Proof of Funds, Buyer Resume, and straightforward email.

Remember, make their job easy and be ready for a possible screening call. Some brokers will call you immediately after receiving your initial inquiry—often before they even send the NDA.

This is usually a screening call. The broker will be assessing your competence, identifying what type of buyer you are, and determining if you are a legitimate operational fit for the business.

Answer the phone professionally. Do not pick up if you sound frustrated, are in a loud environment, or if you have dogs barking in the background. Treat this initial touchpoint like an executive interview.

Most importantly, remain authentic. Do not fake a persona or force a relationship to try and win the deal. Present your actual experience and true intentions. If a broker does not appreciate your authentic approach, let the deal go. The right opportunity will present itself without requiring you to compromise who you are.

> ⚠ **Mentor's Warning**
>
> *If a broker has time to call every inquiry, there may be an issue with the business. Ask how long has the business been on the market? Or are there any known issues or concerns I should be aware of?*

Step 11: Review Provided Information Quickly

Once you sign the NDA, you will receive the Confidential Information Memorandum (CIM).

Understand exactly what this document is: **it is a marketing package.** It is not a forensic audit, and it will not tell you every operational secret of the business. It is designed by the broker to highlight the company's strengths, downplay its weaknesses, and provide a 10,000-foot view of the operation.

Your goal is not to verify every penny on the first day. Your goal is to determine if the business model, financial history, and operational structure warrant taking the next step.

Do not get hypnotized by glossy photos and broker jargon. Strip the emotion out of your review and run the opportunity through this definitive checklist.

The No B.S. CIM Evaluation Checklist

1. The Financial Reality Check

- **Run the Test of Reasonableness:** Do this before you read anything else. If the asking price and SBA debt service leave you with an unlivable wage, close the file immediately.
- **Ignore "Pro Forma" Projections:** Brokers love to include charts showing how much money you could make if you double the marketing budget. You are buying the Seller's reality, not their dreams. Base your valuation strictly on the historical data from the past three years.
- **Scrutinize the Add-Backs:** Does the Seller's Discretionary Earnings (SDE) calculation make logical sense? If the broker added back "essential travel" or "advertising" to artificially inflate the profit, mark it as a massive red flag.

Note From The Lender's Desk

Hear me loud and clear on this: ***If cash income is not reported on the business tax returns, it does not matter how much validation, paperwork, or "proof" they***

provide—a bank will completely ignore it. *To an underwriting department, if the government didn't tax it, it legally does not exist. We will never finance a loan against phantom cash flow. If a seller is hiding income from the IRS, they cannot turn around and use that same income to get a loan from a bank. Base your valuation and your offer strictly on what was filed on their tax returns, and never pay a single dollar for unrecorded cash.*

2. Revenue & Risk

- **Look for Consistency:** Does the revenue bounce wildly from year to year, or is it steady? A steady, slightly boring revenue curve is much safer than a business that spiked once due to a lucky, non-recurring contract and is now slowly bleeding out.
- **Identify Customer Concentration:** Does the CIM indicate that one or two clients make up 20% or more of the total revenue? If so, the risk profile is extremely high. If that one client leaves when the ownership changes, your cash flow collapses.

3. Operations & Key Man Dependency

- **Quantify the Owner's Role:** Look closely at the owner's daily duties and hours worked. If the CIM claims the business is "semi-absentee," but the owner holds the primary contractor license and executes all the sales quotes, the CIM is lying.
- **Evaluate Staff Tenure:** Does the business have a general manager or tenured employees running the day-to-day operations? A business with a highly capable, long-term staff drastically reduces your transition risk.
- **Review the Facility/Lease:** Does the business operate out of a highly specialized commercial space? Check if the lease is transferable and how many years remain before you are forced to negotiate new terms.

4. The Seller's True Motivation

- **Validate the Exit:** Why are they selling? Retirement, health issues, or relocation are highly verifiable, logical reasons for a sale. "Pursuing other business interests" immediately after a year of declining revenue is a red flag.

The Next Move: The Targeted Q&A

If the CIM passes the checklist and the opportunity aligns with your parameters, do not immediately demand fifty tax returns and vendor contracts. That happens during Due Diligence.

Instead, draft a targeted list of 5 to 7 high-level questions for the broker.

Ask questions that bridge the gap between the CIM's 10,000-foot view and a formal face-to-face meeting. For example:

- "Can you elaborate on what the owner's typical 40-hour work week looks like?"
- "How much of the inventory valuation is active, salable stock versus obsolete stock?"
- "Are the three key employees aware of the sale, and are they expected to stay?"

Keep your questions strategic. If the broker's answers satisfy your concerns, request an initial meeting with the Seller.

Step 12: The Initial Q&A

After reviewing the CIM, your ultimate goal is simple: determine if the opportunity warrants a formal face-to-face meeting with the Seller.

If the business model and financials align with your parameters, send the broker a short, highly targeted list of initial questions**. Beware: formulating these questions correctly is a test, and many buyers fail it.**

Do not copy and paste a generic list of questions from Google, and do not ask AI to generate a list for you. Brokers review thousands of inquiries. We instantly spot generic, irrelevant questions, and it immediately flags you as a time-wasting amateur.

Furthermore, do not send deep, forensic due diligence questions at this stage. If there is a massive, glaring concern in the CIM, you can ask for high-level clarification, but do not ask the Broker or Seller to spend hours gathering data before you have even submitted an offer.

To guarantee your questions are appropriate for this stage, execute **The 10-Minute Rule**.

Look at the list of questions you are about to email the broker and ask yourself: *"If I owned this business, would it take me more than 10 minutes of effort to answer these?"* If the answer is yes, your questions are too deep. If the answer is no, you are good to go.

Appropriate vs. Too Granular (Applying the Rule)

- **Too Granular (Fails the Rule):** "Please provide a monthly breakdown of sales revenues by service category for the last three years."
    - Why it fails: This requires detailed forensics that the Broker likely does not have on hand, forcing the Seller to spend hours pulling reports.
- **Appropriate (Passes the Rule):** "Roughly what percentage of total revenue comes from service sales versus parts sales? Have you seen any shifts over the last three years?"

- Why it passes: The Seller knows this off the top of their head. It takes ten seconds to answer, provides you with the exact insight you need to understand the revenue model, and verifies the general direction of the business.

Knowing the exact, penny-for-penny sales breakdown by service to compare year-over-year performance is critical, but that verification happens later during formal Due Diligence. Right now, you just need a general idea to see if the business aligns with your targets.

If the broker's answers satisfy your concerns, request the initial meeting with the Seller.

Step 13: The Seller Meeting (First Date)

You reviewed the CIM, the Test of Reasonableness passed, and the broker answered your initial 10-minute questions. If you remain interested, it is time to request the initial Buyer/Seller meeting.

This meeting is the critical pivot point of the transaction. It is your first real opportunity to build a relationship and assess if you actually want to buy the business.

The Hierarchy of the Meeting

How and where you meet matters. Push for an in-person meeting whenever possible. Meeting face-to-face provides a massive competitive advantage. It allows you to build a genuine relationship beyond a sterile email or a legal LOI, significantly increasing the odds of your offer being accepted over a faceless competitor.

Execute this specific hierarchy when scheduling the meeting:

- **In-Person On-Site (The Gold Standard):** Meeting at the actual place of business is ideal so you can observe the operation firsthand. However, due to strict confidentiality, Sellers often reject this to avoid spooking employees.
- **In-Person Off-Site:** If the facility is off-limits, meet at a neutral, private location (like a quiet coffee shop or the broker's office).
- **Video Conference:** If geography or scheduling prevents an in-person meeting, mandate a video call. You need to see each other's facial expressions and body language.
- **Phone Call (The Last Resort):** Only accept a standard phone call if all other options are entirely impossible.

It's a Date, Not an Interrogation

Many buyers step into this meeting completely misunderstanding the purpose. They treat it like a hostile corporate interrogation. They sometimes show up with a clipboard, a defensive attitude, and a list of sixty aggressive financial questions, ready to grill the Seller on minor tax return discrepancies.

Executing the meeting this way is a fatal mistake. **This is not an audit; this is a first date.** Selling a small business is an intensely emotional process. They are terrified of handing the keys over to a buyer who might destroy their legacy, fire their loyal employees, or run the brand into the ground.

If a Seller does not like you, or if they do not trust you, they will not sell to you—even if you offer the full asking price. Your primary objective is to build rapport, establish trust, and prove that you are a highly capable, respectful steward.

The Standard Agenda

When we run these meetings, we follow a specific, proven flow. Expect the meeting to follow this cadence:

- **The Buyer Introduction:** You will start. Since you already know about the Seller from the CIM, you will introduce yourself, detail your operational experience, and state your intentions on why you want to buy their business. This is your opportunity to share why you may be a great fit for their business.
- **The Seller's Journey:** The Seller will then introduce themselves and tell the story of how they built the company and why they are finally ready to sell.
- **The Q&A:** The floor opens for you to ask questions to determine if this opportunity truly aligns with your parameters.

Note that sometimes you may start with a friendly introduction, perform a tour, and then get into the formal steps starting with "The Buyer Introduction".

Rules of Engagement

To win the room, execute these fundamental rules:

- **Dress for the Target:** Do not overdress. If you are looking to buy a blue-collar plumbing business, do not wear a tailored suit; you will instantly make the Seller uncomfortable. Default to clean business casual—respectful, but grounded in reality.

- **Punctuality Discipline:** Arrive exactly on time. Do not be late, but do not arrive 15 minutes early and start the meeting without the broker (a guaranteed way to irritate the professional managing your deal).
- **Prepare Your Pitch:** Be ready to clearly articulate exactly why you want to buy this specific business. Have crisp, confident answers prepared regarding your own background.
- **Go With the Flow:** Keep the conversation natural. Do not pull out a piece of paper and rigidly read down a list of questions. Express continued interest and let the conversation breathe. You can always email follow-up questions the next morning.

Appropriate vs. Too Granular

Do not use this meeting to verify the math. You will have 30 to 45 days during formal Due Diligence to rip the financials apart with your CPA. Use this meeting to understand the operations, the culture, and the owner's daily reality.

Granular questions put the Seller on the defensive; appropriate questions get the Seller talking passionately about the business.

- **Too Granular (Save for Due Diligence):** "Why is line 42 on your 2022 tax return $4,000 different from your Profit and Loss statement?"
- **Appropriate (Ask Now):** "Can you walk me through your relationship with your CPA and how you generally handle your bookkeeping?"
- **Too Granular (Save for Due Diligence):** "I need to see the exact expiration dates and early termination penalties for your facility lease."
- **Appropriate (Ask Now):** "How is your relationship with the landlord, and do you foresee any issues keeping the business in this location long-term?"

The Formal Question Bank

To control the room and command respect, ask open-ended questions that let the Seller shine. A street-smart buyer listens 80% of the time and speaks 20% of the time.

Select 5 to 7 questions from the following categories to guide the conversation:

- **The Owner's Reality:** "What does a typical day look like for you? What time do you arrive, and what are your primary daily duties?"
- **The Best and Worst:** "What is the absolute best part of owning this business, and what is the part you will be happiest to leave behind?"
- **Key Man Dependency:** "If you were forced to leave for a month-long vacation tomorrow, what would break first?"
- **The Team:** "Who is your most irreplaceable employee, and what exactly makes them so valuable?"
- **Growth:** "What is the biggest bottleneck currently holding the business back from doubling its revenue?"
- **Advice for the Buyer:** "If you were in my shoes, buying this business today, what would you focus entirely on during the first 90 days?"

> ⚠ **Mentor's Warning: The "Fixer" Ego Trap**
>
> *Never sit across from a Seller and list all the things you plan to "fix," "disrupt," or "modernize" on day one. Even if their software is twenty years old and their marketing is completely nonexistent, keep your mouth shut unless asked. Telling a Seller their systems are obsolete insults their life's work.Instead, deploy this exact script: "You have built an incredible foundation here. My goal is to learn everything I can from you during the transition so I can simply continue the great work you've started."*

Once the meeting concludes, immediately evaluate your gut feeling. Do you trust this Seller? Do you believe their operational narrative matches the CIM? If the answer is yes, it is time to deploy the template LOI you built in Step 5 and lock the business down.

Step 14: Submit the LOI (Strike with Speed)

If the initial meeting went well, your questions were answered, and your gut tells you this is the right business, do not hesitate. It is time to deploy the Letter of Intent you prepared in Step 5.

In the acquisition battlefield, speed is a weapon. You built your LOI template for this exact moment. Do not wait a week to "think about it," and absolutely do not wait for a lawyer to draft a document from scratch.

Customize the Variables

Open your pre-reviewed LOI template and make the deal-specific adjustments based on what you learned in the meeting.

- **The Purchase Price:** Insert your offer based on your Test of Reasonableness, the financials, and risks and benefits you learned during the meeting.
- **The Transition Period:** Tailor the transition timeline specifically to what you and the Seller discussed during the meeting. (If they mentioned they want to stay on for 60 days to ensure a smooth handoff, write exactly 60 days into the LOI) unless absolutely needed otherwise.
- **The Deal Structure:** Insert your specific down payment, the SBA loan contingency, and the required Seller Financing percentages.

Eliminate the Competition

By submitting a clean, professional LOI within 24 hours of your initial meeting, you completely outmaneuver the competition.

While another potential buyer is stuck trading emails with their attorney trying to figure out how to draft an offer, your document is already sitting on the broker's desk. You prove your extreme competence, validate your financial readiness, and apply immediate, tangible pressure to the Seller.

The Expiration Clock

Never submit an open-ended offer. If you hand a broker an LOI without a deadline, they could use your offer as leverage to create a bidding war with other buyers. To prevent this, put a hard expiration clock on your LOI to try and have them commit to your LOI before others get a chance to submit theirs.

Include a clear clause that states: *"This Letter of Intent is valid until 5:00 PM CST on [Date 48 to 72 hours from submission]. If not executed by the Seller by this deadline, this offer is automatically withdrawn."* Setting a 48-to-72-hour expiration forces the Seller to make a decision. They cannot sit on your offer for two weeks. It forces a "Yes," a "No," or a formal counter-offer, immediately locking out the slower tourists who are still trying to find their pens.

Submit the LOI, set the clock, and prepare for negotiations.

Step 15: Negotiate the LOI and Execute

You submitted the LOI and set the expiration clock. The pressure is formally on the Seller.

Now, you must manage your expectations. Unless you offered the full asking price with zero Seller Financing, do not expect an immediate signature. Prepare for a counter-offer.

Sellers are emotionally tied to their businesses, and human psychology dictates that they want to feel like they "won" the negotiation. A street-smart buyer understands this dynamic and actively lets the Seller win the battles that do not fundamentally break the deal.

- **Trade Price for Terms** When the broker returns with the Seller's counter-offer, it will almost always focus on the purchase price. If a Seller demands a higher price, do not blindly concede. Trade price for terms.

  If you agree to increase your offer by **$25,000** to close the gap, require the Seller to finance that exact **$25,000** on a standby note, or ask for an additional 30 days of transitional training at no cost.

- **Drop Your Ego (The Penny Trap)** This is the phase where arrogant buyers blow up life-changing opportunities.

  Know your absolute "walk-away" number before the broker ever calls you back. If the Seller's counter-offer pushes the math beyond your Test of Reasonableness, politely decline and walk away.

  However, if the math still works, drop your ego. I watch buyers fight to the death over **$25,000** on a **$1,500,000** acquisition that generates **$500,000** a year in free cash flow. They get deeply offended that the Seller countered them, and they dig their heels in purely out of pride.

  Do not trip over pennies on your way to millions. If the business is an exceptional asset, and the counter-offer still comfortably clears your debt service requirements, accept the counter and secure the asset. You will recoup that $25,000 in future NOI. Think bigger!

- **Execute and Secure Exclusivity** Once you and the Seller reach a verbal agreement on the final terms, update the LOI document immediately. Do not wait for the broker to do it; drive the process yourself.

  Send the updated LOI for electronic signature. The exact moment both you and the Seller sign that document, the dynamic of the transaction fundamentally shifts.

You officially enter **Exclusivity**. The "No Shop" or "Exclusivity" clause activates. The Seller legally cannot entertain, discuss, or accept backup offers from the dozens of other buyers circling the deal. The business is officially off the market, and the asset is protected during your review of the opportunity.

Take a breath and celebrate for exactly five minutes. The hunt is over, but the war is about to begin. You must now pivot from being a salesperson to being an investigator. It is time for Due Diligence.

Step 16: Rubber Meets the Road (Executing Due Diligence) — Works Concurrent with Step 17

You secured exclusivity. The 30-day clock starts right now. Welcome to trench warfare.

This is where the rubber meets the road. Your objective is simple: ask for everything and verify that every single claim presented in the CIM is true and accurate. Your ultimate goal is to dig up any hidden skeletons before your initial 30-day due diligence period expires. If you uncover a catastrophic lie or finding during this window, you can terminate the LOI and walk away without losing a single cent.

To prevent yourself from drowning in paperwork, you must manage this process systematically. Do not just blindly ask for documents. Execute a structured, chronological plan.

The 30-Day Execution Timeline

Manage the clock ruthlessly. Execute your diligence in these four distinct phases to ensure nothing slips through the cracks:

- Days 1–3 (**The Kickoff & Data Request**): Deliver your formal, comprehensive document request list to the broker. Establish a secure Virtual Data Room (VDR) using a platform like Google Drive or Dropbox. Organize the VDR into clean folders (Financials, Legal, Operations, Employees) so the Seller can upload documents systematically. Introduce your CPA and Attorney to the broker to establish direct lines of communication and access to the VDR.

- Days 4–15 (**Financial Forensics**): Focus entirely on the math. Immediately begin associating the tax returns, Profit & Loss statements, and bank statements. Do not move on to reviewing the facility lease or the equipment if the financial math is broken and not adding up. If you do, you may be wasting energy if the financials are not accurate and the deal falls through because of it.

> 👁 **Note From The Lender's Desk**
>
> *Send this financial info to your lender right away. Get the process rolling!*

- Days 16–25 (**Operational & Legal Audit**): Once the financials pass verification, pivot to operations. Learn everything you can about the business model, employees, services, products, and so forth. Execute site visits to inspect equipment. Have your attorney review the facility lease, vendor contracts, and run the UCC lien searches.

- Days 26–30 (**The Go/No-Go Decision**): Synthesize all findings. Did the business pass? If yes, formally request the first extension of exclusivity to finalize the bank loan and the Definitive Agreement. If you uncovered a massive, unacceptable lie or just plain inaccuracies, either execute your termination rights and walk away or renegotiate the terms to meet the accurate findings.

Lean on Your Forensic Team: In most cases, it is recommended not to attempt financial due diligence by yourself unless you are a highly experienced accountant. I recommend you hire a professional to assist. You need to be certain the business is performing as presented to protect yourself.

How you deploy those professionals depends entirely on the size of the deal:

- **The CPA Review:** If you are buying a $200,000 to $999,000 business, hire a sharp, transaction-experienced CPA to review the tax returns, balance sheets, Profit and Loss Statements and bank statements.
- **The Quality of Earnings Report (For Large Deals):** If you are acquiring a business valued over $1,000,000, commission a formal Quality of Earnings (QoE) report from a third-party financial firm. A QoE is a deep, forensic audit that verifies the exact sustainability of the cash flow and validates every single add-back. Paying $10,000 to $20,000 for a QoE on a small $200,000 business makes zero mathematical sense. But on a $2,000,000 acquisition, skipping a QoE is financial suicide.

Note From The Lender's Desk

There ***is absolutely no accepted universal standard for a QoE report.***

To be completely blunt, any random person can spin up a website over the weekend, make up a handful of official-sounding credentials, and start charging unsuspecting buyers thousands of dollars for QoE work. There is zero licensing, zero regulatory oversight, and zero credentialing requirements to enter the QoE space.

If you are going to spend the money on a QoE, you must ensure the provider is running an underwriting-grade analysis. Before you sign an engagement letter with an accounting firm, ask your SBA lender for their approved ***Scope of Work (SOW)****. If your lender doesn't have one handy, ensure your chosen CPA firm includes these four non-negotiable pillars in their SOW, or the bank will not accept it:*

- ***Tax Return Reconciliation:*** *A granular, line-by-line reconciliation proving that the numbers in the general ledger exactly match the final, filed federal corporate tax returns.*
- ***Proof of Cash:*** *A complete verification matching the company's stated revenues against actual historical bank statements, ensuring no "phantom invoicing" is taking place.*
- ***The Working Capital Peg:*** *A strict calculation of the historical net working capital required to run the business month-to-month, giving the bank a definitive number to build into the loan.*
- ***Customer & Vendor Concentration Analysis:*** *A clear breakdown proving that a single customer or supplier doesn't account for more than 15% to 20% of total company revenue or materials.*

Do not let a vendor write their own easy checklist. Bring your bank's expected scope to the table first, ensure a qualified CPA handles the file, and save yourself from a catastrophic rejection during underwriting.

The Bank as a Secondary Shield

If you finance the transaction through an SBA 7(a) loan, the bank acts as your secondary safety net. The bank absolutely will not lend millions of dollars on a business that is failing, heavily overvalued, or buried in legal liabilities. They conduct their own parallel diligence, demand an independent third-party business valuation, and search for liens. However, never rely solely on the bank. You are the CEO of this transaction; drive the diligence yourself.

The No B.S. Due Diligence Checklist

Provide your CPA and Attorney with all provided documents, and request any documents they request along with the following items from the Seller to validate the business across three major categories:

1. Financial Validation (Follow the Cash)

- Bank Statements vs. Tax Returns: Match the monthly bank statement deposits and expenses directly against the filed tax returns and the P&L. The Golden Rule of Diligence: If the cash did not physically hit the business bank account, it does not exist. Never pay a multiple on undocumented "under-the-table" cash.
- Verify Add-Backs: Demand receipts and invoices for every single add-back claimed in the Seller's Discretionary Earnings (SDE) calculation. If they claim a $12,000 personal travel add-back, request the receipts associated to that trip to ensure it truly was a personal expense.

👁 Note From The Lender's Desk

Just because a seller can produce a physical paper receipt for an expense does not mean the bank is going to automatically accept it as a legitimate addback.

*Standard categories like **Meals, Entertainment, Travel, Cell Phones, and Personal Utilities** are almost universally **blanket declined** as addbacks at every bank I have ever worked at.*

Underwriters look at those categories and safely assume that you, the new owner, will inevitably have your own version of those exact same operational expenses just to keep the business running and client relationships healthy. If a broker's SDE calculation is heavily propped up by adding back the seller's steak dinners, family road trips, and phone upgrades, strip those out of your valuation models immediately. If the bank won't lend against it, you shouldn't pay for it.

- Accounts Receivable (A/R) Aging Report: Identify exactly who owes the business money and how late they are. A massive A/R balance filled with invoices past 90 days indicates customers who will never pay.
- Accounts Payable (A/P) Report: Identify exactly who the business owes money to. Ensure the Seller is paying vendors on time and not artificially inflating their cash flow by ignoring bills.
- Review Point of Sale (POS) Data: If you are buying a retail or restaurant business, requests reports directly from the POS software (like Square or Toast) to verify daily transaction volume matches the P&L.

2. Legal & SBA Requirements (Check for Skeletons)

- UCC Lien Search: Your attorney must run a Uniform Commercial Code (UCC) search. This verifies whether the Seller pledged any business equipment or assets as collateral for undisclosed loans. The Seller must clear all liens prior to or at closing.
- Tax Clearance Letters: Require state and federal tax clearance letters to prove the Seller does not owe back taxes. If you buy the assets of a business with outstanding sales tax liabilities, the state can hold you responsible.
- Pending Litigation: Demand a formal, signed disclosure stating there are no active, pending, or threatened lawsuits against the business, the entity, or the owner.
- Employee Verification (I-9s and W-2s): Verify that all employees are legally authorized to work and are properly classified. A business heavily relying on misclassified "1099 Independent Contractors" to avoid paying payroll taxes and workers' compensation carries a massive legal liability.

3. Operational Diligence (Protecting the Future)

- **The Facility Lease:** This kills more deals than bad financials. Demand a copy of the current lease immediately. Does it expire in three months? Does the landlord have a "demolition clause" allowing them to tear down the building? Verify that the lease is fully transferable to you, or secure a written commitment from the landlord for a new, favorable lease.

- **Vendor Contracts & Pricing:** Verify that the current pricing the Seller receives from primary suppliers transfers to you. If the Seller relies on a "handshake deal" with their brother-in-law for cheap materials, your margins will instantly collapse post-sale.
- **Customer Concentration Validation:** Cross-reference the sales reports. Verify that no single customer accounts for a dangerous percentage of total revenue (typically anything over 15% to 20%).
- **Equipment Inspection:** Do not just read the Asset List; physically inspect the equipment. If the CIM claims a fleet of five trucks, verify that all five trucks run, have current registrations, possess maintenance logs, and are not sitting on blocks in the back lot.

Note From The Lender's Desk

When you are performing your initial review of a company's asset list and physical facility, you must determine what kind of equipment upgrades or structural improvements you will realistically be staring down in the next two to five years. If you don't calculate those future capital expenditures into your macro modeling today, a single broken HVAC unit or a failing delivery truck can instantly wipe out your early profits. Budget for the transition, protect your liquidity, and ensure you leave yourself a healthy financial runway.

Mentor's Warning

During Due Diligence, you will find discrepancies. No small business possesses Perfect books. "Retrading" is the act of trying to lower the purchase price at the 11th hour because of a minor finding.If you find a massive $100,000 lie, you must renegotiate or walk away. But if you find a $1,500 accounting error on a highly profitable $1,000,000 business, let it go. Do not irritate the Seller and risk losing a life-changing asset because your ego demands a minor discount. Protect the macro prize.

Step 17: Concurrent Execution (Financing & Legal)

Do not wait for Due Diligence to end before you secure a pre-approval from the bank and begin drafting your contracts. If you sit on your hands for 30 days and then call your banker, your deal will stall, exclusivity will expire, and the Seller will get irritated.

While your CPA is in the trenches running the financial forensics (Step 16), you must simultaneously drive two parallel tracks: securing the bank's Term Sheet and drafting the Definitive Agreement.

Track 1: Secure the Term Sheet (The Rule of Three)

Roughly one to two weeks into your 30-day Due Diligence window—once you are confident the initial financials are holding up—activate the lenders you pre-qualified with back in Step 3.

Your objective is to secure a formal Term Sheet before your 30-day exclusivity expires. A Term Sheet is the bank's official proposal outlining the loan amount, interest rate, equity injection requirement, and repayment schedule. If a lender issues a Term Sheet, you are highly likely to receive final approval, provided no hidden skeletons emerge during final underwriting.

Execute the Rule of Three. Submit the deal structure to two or three lenders simultaneously.

Running multiple lenders provides two massive advantages:

- **Leverage:** You can compare the Term Sheets side-by-side to ensure you are securing the absolute best rates and deal terms.
- **Protection:** It is incredibly common for one bank's underwriting department to say "no" while another says "yes." If you put all your faith in one lender and they reject the deal on Day 25, you lose a month of progress and likely lose the business. Running parallel lenders guarantees you always have a backup plan ready to deploy.

Note From The Lender's Desk

Assuming you have gotten yourself personally prequalified, a seasoned lender should be able to look at a live deal and give you a pretty quick **"No."** *To get that rapid baseline assessment you need to provide the below items:*

- ***The CIM and Addback Schedule***
- ***Past 3 Years of Corporate Tax Return***
- ***YTD P&L and Balance Sheet***
- ***A Draft LOI (Letter of Intent)***

Track 2: Draft the Definitive Agreement

The Definitive Agreement is the master contract that legally binds the transaction. It is typically structured as an **Asset Purchase Agreement (APA)** or, less commonly, an **Equity Purchase Agreement (EPA)**.

Timing is everything here. Do not pay an attorney a massive retainer to draft a 40-page contract on Day 1 of Due Diligence. If your CPA finds out on Day 5 that the Seller lied about their revenue, you just burned thousands of dollars in legal fees for a dead deal.

Wait until you are deep enough into Due Diligence to possess absolute confidence that the business is solid. Usually, around Day 25, once the financials are verified and the major operational risks are cleared, pull the trigger.

Instruct your Business Attorney to draft the initial Definitive Agreement. By initiating the legal drafting before the 30-day DD period concludes, you position yourself to smoothly transition out of exclusivity and directly into the final closing procedures without losing momentum.

Step 18: Negotiate The Final Binding Purchase Agreement

Once you deliver the initial draft of the Definitive Agreement to the Seller, expect their counsel to take one to two weeks to respond.

More importantly, expect a sea of red ink and an emotional roller coaster.

No matter how many times you instruct your attorney to draft a "fair and balanced" agreement, the first draft will inherently favor you, the Buyer. The Seller's attorney will counter by striking out your protections and heavily favoring the Seller. This is standard legal posturing. Do not panic, and do not take the redlines personally.

The Two-Turn Rule

Allow the attorneys to handle the first two "turns" (revisions) of the agreement between themselves. They need this space to argue the standard legal boilerplate.

However, if they reach an impasse over specific clauses after the second turn, step in immediately. Do not let two attorneys wage a billing-hour war over a minor clause. Attorneys do not always play nice, and they rarely provide the opposing side with the actual business rationale behind their demands.

If negotiations stall, instruct the Broker to arrange a direct call between you and the Seller (with or without the attorneys present). When one business owner hears the logical rationale of the other, they almost always find a compromise.

Remember: You are the CEO of this transaction. Your attorney works for you. You sign their checks. If they are over-lawyering a minor point and jeopardizing the asset, order them to concede and move forward.

> ⚠ **Mentor's Warning**
>
> *As of today, be incredibly cautious using Artificial Intelligence to write or review your definitive agreements. AI is a fantastic tool for analyzing CIMs or brainstorming interview questions, but in legal contracts, a single hallucinated word or missing comma can cost you hundreds of thousands of dollars. Pay a human professional to finalize the legal text.*

Common Battlegrounds (And How to Create Win-Wins)

Whether you are executing an Asset Purchase Agreement (APA) or an Equity Purchase Agreement (EPA), the attorneys will predictably fight over the same five deal points. Anticipate these discrepancies and deploy these win-win solutions to keep the deal alive:

1. Indemnification: Caps and Baskets

- **The Conflict:** You want the Seller completely liable for any undisclosed issues that pop up after closing (lawsuits, unpaid taxes). You want this protection to last forever. The Seller wants a clean break on closing day and zero future liability.
- **The Win-Win:** Establish a "Basket" (a deductible) and a "Cap" (a maximum limit). Agree that the Seller is not responsible for minor nuisance claims under $10,000 (the Basket), but if a massive issue arises, their maximum liability is up to the total purchase price (the Cap). Limit the survival period of this clause to 24 to 36 months, giving you two–three full audit cycles to find any hidden issues. (Note: Exceptions are made for fundamental reps and warranties such as fraud or intentional tax evasion, which should carry infinite liability).

2. Target Working Capital (Heavy in EPAs)

- **The Conflict:** If you are buying the entity (EPA) or acquiring Accounts Receivable in an APA, you need enough cash left in the business on day one to make payroll and pay rent. The Seller wants to sweep all the cash out of the bank accounts at the closing table.

- **The Win-Win:** Establish a "Working Capital Peg." Calculate the historical 12-month average of the working capital required to run the business. Require the Seller to leave exactly that amount in the business at closing. If they leave more, you pay them the difference. If they leave less, you deduct the shortfall from the final purchase price.

> 👁 **Note From The Lender's Desk**
>
> *When you are structuring your offer, make sure to ask your SBA lender early on how they handle including a cash working capital allocation directly inside the acquisition loan itself.*

3. Purchase Price Allocation (APA Specific)

- **The Conflict:** In an Asset Sale, the IRS requires you to allocate the purchase price across different asset classes (Equipment, Inventory, Goodwill). You want to allocate heavily to fast-depreciating assets (like Equipment) to lower your immediate tax burden. The Seller wants to allocate heavily to Goodwill to secure a lower capital gains tax rate.
- **The Win-Win:** This is a zero-sum tax game. Have both CPAs run the tax implications. Meet in the middle. If the Seller takes a slightly higher tax hit to accommodate your allocation request, offset their pain by bumping the Seller Financing interest rate up by half a point.

4. The Non-Compete Scope

- **The Conflict:** You want to legally ban the Seller from working in your industry, anywhere in the country, for ten years. The Seller wants a one-year ban limited to a five-mile radius.
- **The Win-Win:** Tie the geography strictly to the actual footprint where the business currently operates and pulls revenue. Limit the timeframe to the standard SBA max or reasonable industry standard (typically 3 to

5 years). A judge will throw out an overly aggressive non-compete anyway; make it fair and legally enforceable.

5. Post-Closing Transition and Consulting

- **The Conflict:** You want the Seller chained to their desk for six months to ensure you don't fail. The Seller wants to move to a beach in Florida the day after closing.
- **The Win-Win:** Agree to 30–90 days of full-time, inclusive support to execute the immediate operational handoff. After an agreed period of in-person support, transition the Seller to an independent consultant. Offer to pay them a premium hourly rate for phone and email support for up to six months more. This gives you a safety net while respecting the Seller's retirement time.

Address these five battlegrounds quickly and logically. Once the redlines stop and both parties agree to the terms, you have successfully locked in the Definitive Agreement.

You are now in the home stretch.

Step 19: Closing the Deal & The Post Close Handoff

As the Definitive Agreement gets finalized and the bank's underwriting department issues their formal approval, you enter the final phase of the acquisition.

This is the last major push to get to the closing table. Be prepared: the final mile of an acquisition is chaotic and highly stressful. Both the bank and the attorneys are going to hit you with a massive wave of administrative tasks. Expect it, embrace the grind, and push through to the finish line.

The Bank's Final Gauntlet

Before the bank wires millions of dollars to acquire a business, they must bulletproof their collateral and check all their boxes. During the final two weeks before closing, the bank will require several critical items to clear the deal to fund:

- **Collateral Assignment of Life Insurance:** The bank needs a guarantee that they will be repaid if something tragic happens to you. They will require you to take out a life insurance policy matching the loan amount and assign the bank as the primary beneficiary. Get the medical exam done early so this doesn't delay closing.
- **Tax Clearances & Transcripts:** The bank will require the Seller to sign IRS Form 4506-C, authorizing the bank to pull direct tax transcripts from the IRS to ensure the returns provided match reality. They will also require a state "Certificate of No Tax Due" to ensure no sales or franchise taxes are owed.
- **UCC Lien Searches:** The bank will execute their final searches to ensure the Seller's assets are free and clear of undisclosed debt.
- **Landlord Consent and Lease Assignment:** If the business occupies a commercial space, the landlord must formally agree to transfer the lease to your newly formed LLC. The bank will not fund the loan if you do not have legal rights to operate in the building.

- **Business Insurance Policies:** The bank will require comprehensive commercial liability, property, and workers' comp policies to protect their collateral. **Pro-tip:** Ask your bank's designated closing officer if they are open to connecting *directly* with your commercial insurance agent via email. Cutting yourself out as the middleman allows the bank and the agent to trade technical compliance acronyms directly, saving you from an endless, exhausting game of telephone.
- **Franchise Documents (If Applicable):** If you are buying into a franchise network, the bank cannot fund the loan until they review the finalized Franchise Agreement, the Franchise Disclosure Document (FDD), and a signed **Franchise Comfort Letter** from the corporate brand. Corporate franchise legal teams move notoriously slow, so loop them in on day one.
- **Operating Company (OpCo) Legal Docs:** This means the formal legal formation documents for the new corporate entity *you* are spinning up to buy the business (LLC or C-Corp). Underwriters will demand your Articles of Organization, formal Operating Agreement or Bylaws, and your IRS-issued EIN letter. The bank needs to see exactly who owns the borrowing entity down to the penny.
- **The Seller's Equipment List:** This is a granular, itemized inventory list of every single physical asset, vehicle, and piece of machinery included in the purchase price. The closing team will cross-reference this list against active **UCC lien filings** to ensure the seller legally owns this equipment free and clear, and that the bank can successfully attach their security interest to it at closing.

The Closing Document Stack (What You Will Actually Sign)

Part of the closing process involves finalizing the Definitive Agreement and drafting the supplemental legal documents. Because these ancillary documents simply execute the terms you already fought over and agreed to in the APA, they are much easier to finalize.

When it is time to sign, you will be presented with a mountain of paperwork. Here is exactly what is in that stack:

- **The Definitive Agreement (APA or EPA):** The master contract, finalized with all "Schedules" and "Exhibits." Schedules are the detailed lists attached to the back of the agreement (e.g., Schedule A: The exact list of equipment being sold; Schedule B: The list of excluded personal assets).
- **The Bill of Sale:** This is the actual legal "receipt." It formally transfers the ownership of the physical and intangible assets from the Seller's entity to your entity.
- **The Promissory Note & Security Agreement:** If you negotiated Seller Financing, this is the legal loan document dictating your payment terms, interest rate, and the collateral the Seller can claim if you default.
- **The Non-Compete Agreement:** A standalone document legally barring the Seller from opening a competing business within your agreed-upon timeframe and radius.
- **The Transition & Consulting Agreement:** The formal contract dictating exactly how many hours, days, or months the Seller is required to stay on to train you, and what their compensation will be after the initial free transition period ends.
- **The Settlement Statement (Closing Statement):** Prepared by either the closing attorney, escrow agent or the bank. This is the ultimate accounting document. It shows exactly where every penny of the purchase price, bank loan, down payment, and closing fees is going. Review this line-by-line before signing.

The Closing and The Keys

Once the massive stack of paper is signed (which is almost entirely done digitally via DocuSign today), you authorize your bank to wire the loan funds to the appropriate accounts. They will distribute the funds to the Seller, and any of the Seller's debts that need to be paid off to release a lien.

Congratulations. You own a business.

The Post-Close Handoff (Day One)

The transaction is closed, but the transition has just begun. Day One as the new owner is critical to the long-term survival of the business. Execute the handoff with precision and empathy.

- **The Employee Announcement:** Do not walk into the building on Monday morning and announce that you are the new boss. The Seller must introduce you. Have the Seller gather the team, express their gratitude for their hard work, explain that they are retiring/moving on, and personally endorse you as the hand-picked successor who is going to protect their jobs and keep the culture alive.
- **Observe, Do Not Disrupt:** The fastest way to trigger a mass exodus of key employees is to immediately change the rules. Do not change the software, do not change the payroll schedule, and do not reorganize the dispatch routes on your first week. Your only job for the first 30 days is to observe, learn, and prove to the staff that their paychecks are safe.
- **The Digital Transfer:** Sit down with the Seller and transfer the "keys." This means migrating the admin rights of the domain names, website hosting, software platforms, social media accounts, utilities, and primary vendor accounts into your name.
- **Merchant Accounts:** Ensure your new credit card processing systems and business bank accounts are live and fully integrated so you do not miss a single dollar of revenue on your first day of operations.

You have successfully navigated the gauntlet. Now, the real work begins.

Step 20: Transitioning In Detail

The wire has cleared, the ink is dry, and the keys are in your pocket. You successfully navigated the gauntlet of buying a business which is no easy task as you know.

Before you step fully into the CEO role, you must execute a few final, critical strategies to protect your investment and ensure your transition is a success. Buying the business was just the prerequisite; now you have to run it.

Archive the War Chest (Your Legal Shield)

Over my decade of executing these transactions, I have learned one absolute operational law: save everything.

Take the original CIM, the email threads, the financial statements, the Q&A transcripts, and the final Definitive Agreement, and lock them in a secure digital archive. Do not delete a single communication you had with the Seller or the broker prior to closing.

I pray you never need to look at these documents again. However, if you take over and discover six months later that a massive vendor contract was fabricated, or the Seller lied about pending litigation, this archive is your legal ammunition. You need past records not just to reference historical operations, but to enforce the Indemnification clauses you fought so hard for in Step 18. Keep the paper trail bulletproof.

Mastering Day One: The Employee Flight Risk

The number one fear every buyer has is: *"What if all the employees quit the day I take over?"*

It is a valid concern, but you must understand the nuances. If the staff consists entirely of the Seller's family members, lifelong best friends, or transient independent contractors, the flight risk is massive. That is a major red flag you should have priced into the deal during Due Diligence.

However, if the staff consists of standard, hardworking W-2 employees, their retention depends entirely on you.

In most cases, the Seller has kept the sale strictly confidential. The team will likely find out about the acquisition on your first day, or mere hours before you arrive. They will be shocked, and their immediate, internal reaction will be panic. Will I lose my job? Will my pay be cut? Are my benefits changing?

The Retention Playbook

Your objective on Day One is to extinguish that panic immediately. Start the relationship on the right foot by leading with respect and absolute stability.

- **The Reassurance:** Address the team alongside the Seller. Look them in the eye and guarantee that nothing is changing overnight. Tell them you bought the business because of them—because they built a great culture and a profitable operation.
- **The Strategic Raise:** If the cash flow permits, consider initiating a small, unexpected raise or a "stay bonus" for key personnel during your first few weeks. It is a powerful gesture that instantly proves you are invested in their success and well-being.
- **Be a Decent Human:** Put yourself in their shoes. If a new boss walks in, respects your institutional knowledge, listens to your concerns, and actively wants to help you grow, you are not going to quit. If an arrogant new boss walks in, talks down to you, and treats you like a line item on a spreadsheet, you will start updating your resume that afternoon. Command respect by giving it.

The 60-Day Operational Freeze

Once introductions are done, your job title is not "Disruptor." Your job title is "Sponge."

Learn everything you can before considering even the smallest change. Institute a mandatory 60-Day Operational Freeze. Unless there is a catastrophic emergency or an immediate safety hazard, do not change the software, do not overhaul the marketing, and do not change the breakroom coffee brand for two full months.

When you do identify an area for improvement, run the proposed idea by the Seller or your tenured employees first. Never tear down a fence until you know exactly why it was built in the first place. There may be a highly specific, historical reason a process is done a certain way—a reason that saves the company time and money.

Remember, you bought this business because it was already successful. Respect the foundation. Become a complete expert in the daily operations first, and then implement your improvements once you truly grasp the mechanics of the machine.

The Reality of Grit

Lastly, you must accept a hard truth: owning a business is incredibly difficult, especially in the beginning.

The spreadsheets look clean, but reality is messy. You are going to be tested. You will face unexpected equipment failures, difficult customers, and days where you question why you ever left the safety of your corporate cubicle. Be prepared to work grueling hours and sacrifice your comfort.

To survive and ultimately thrive, you must possess grit. When you get knocked down, you have to get back up immediately.

You will make mistakes. You will misquote a job, mishandle an employee conflict, or waste money on a bad marketing campaign. This is normal. A mistake is only a failure if you refuse to learn from it. Otherwise, consider that lost money the "tuition" you pay to learn how to be a CEO. Pay the tuition, learn the lesson, and do not look back. It will get easier over time as your experience and tolerance grows.

You have the playbook. You know the rules of engagement. Now, go execute.

Chapter 7 | The Final Cheat Sheet: Red Flags, Broker Secrets, and The Bottom Line

If you have made it this far, you possess the exact playbook required to acquire a highly profitable business. You know the math, you know the process, and you know how to protect yourself.

But deals are not done in a safe room. They involve highly emotional sellers, protective brokers, and the messy reality of human nature. Before I send you out into the market, I am emptying my desk.

What follows is the raw, unfiltered truth from over a decade of brokering deals and selling four of my own. Consider this your final cheat sheet—the ultimate list of Do's, Don'ts, Things You Should Know and Deal-Killers to keep you safe in the trenches.

Things You Should Know: The Absolute Do's and Don'ts

- **DON'T ever value a business on "future potential."** If a Seller or Broker tries to justify a massive asking price by pointing to all the "future possibilities" (e.g., "If you just build a website, sales will double!"), walk away. Possibilities are great—they are the reason you buy the business—but you do not pay the Seller for work you are going to do. Value is based strictly on historical performance. You pay for their reality; you profit from your improvements.
- **DO trust your gut.** If something smells fishy, it's fishy. The human brain is incredibly good at subconsciously picking up on micro-inconsistencies. If you get a bad vibe, feeling, or if the financials feel manipulated, do not brush it off. Trust your instincts and dig deeper.
- **DON'T ever send an LOI blindly.** Never submit a formal offer without meeting the Seller in person or over a video call. A business is essentially a living organism driven by its owner. If you don't look them in the eye and assess their character, you have no idea what you are actually

buying. Additionally, a good Broker is not only trying to find a buyer with money, but someone who is a good fit. Meeting is your opportunity to demonstrate that.

- **DON'T let the Seller broadcast the sale early.** Do not let the Seller send out an email blast to their clients or employees saying, "I just sold the business!" before or immediately after closing. This creates massive panic and can instantly harm operations. If a Seller is eager to do this, ask them why. It is often a red flag that they are trying to dump the business and run. The transition must be a carefully orchestrated, in-person handoff.

- **DO attach your Pre-Qualification to your Proof of Funds.** We discussed Proof of Funds in the playbook, but if you want to be the ultimate top-tier prospect, attach a pre-qualification letter from your SBA lender alongside your Proof of Funds. This tells the broker you are fully loaded, weapons hot, and ready to close.

- **DON'T Expect To Meet The Employees.** In most cases, this is a typical no-go, however, there are circumstances that require it. If there is a critical key employee, or a seller that cannot perform a suitable transition/consulting period post sale, then an employee meeting/introduction may make sense. Again, if it's a reasonable request beyond emotion, most Sellers will understand and can possibly occur the week of closing. However, this is not typical for sub $5,000,000 deals. I would say only 35% of the transactions allow Buyers to meet employees pre-close.

- **DON'T Schedule a Closing on Friday.** Make every effort to not allow the bank or broker to schedule your transactional closing on a Friday. Bank wire cutoffs are ruthlessly unforgiving. If any minor document error, signature omission, or administrative hiccup occurs at 3:00 PM on a Friday, the funds will fail to clear before the weekend. This throws both you and the Seller into an uncomfortable position and emotional limbo state over the weekend. The legal paperwork is fully signed, but the financial consideration has not been received. Not a good position to be in, even if temporary.

The Deal-Killers (Big Red Flags)

When reviewing a listing or sitting in a Seller meeting, keep your radar up for these massive red flags. If you spot them, proceed with extreme caution or run.

- **The Young "Retiree":** If a 35-year-old owner says they are selling to "retire," be highly skeptical. They are either completely burned out (meaning the business is a meat grinder) or they see a massive industry threat looming on the horizon and are trying to cash out before the ship sinks.
- **The "Other Business" Excuse:** An owner selling because they "want to focus on another business" is screaming one of two things: "This business is not worth my time anymore," or "This business is not as profitable as I am presenting."
- **Voodoo Accounting:** This is when a business shows a Net Ordinary Loss on its tax returns, but the broker or seller creatively adds back "unique" expenses to magically show a massive profit. If you see a Net Ordinary Income loss and unusual add-backs, proceed cautiously.
- **Overly Complicated Models:** Complexity equals risk. Most great, cash-flowing Main Street businesses do not require a degree in rocket science to understand. If you cannot explain how the business makes money to a fifth-grader, I probably wouldn't buy it.
- **The Stale Listing:** If a highly profitable-looking business has been sitting on the market for nine months, there is usually a reason. A dozen other buyers have likely looked under the hood and found a fatal flaw the broker isn't advertising.
- **The Hit-and-Run Seller:** An owner who refuses to sign a transition agreement or provide at least 30 days of post-sale support is usually hiding skeletons unless it's a super simple business model or a full team is in place.
- **The Unicorn Paradox:** An owner who is making a massive amount of money, supposedly working minimal hours, and still wants to sell. If it's

that easy and that lucrative, they would keep it. It is almost always too good to be true.

- **The Nightmare Negotiator:** Pay close attention to how the Seller acts during the initial Q&A or LOI phase. If they are aggressively difficult, petty, or evasive in the beginning, they are going to be an absolute nightmare when you get into the hard trenches of formal Due Diligence.

Confessions from the Broker's Desk (The Insider Secrets)

You deserve to know how the other side of the table operates. Understanding the broker's motivations will make you a far superior negotiator.

Secret #1: Brokers usually get a referral fee from lenders.

This isn't a dirty secret, but you need to be aware of it. If a broker pushes you hard to use "their guy" at a specific bank, they are likely getting a kickback. However, this isn't necessarily a bad thing. I get referrals, but I can confidently say the lenders my firm recommends are genuinely the best in the business. They are highly responsive and work for banks that actually want to close deals.The Play: If a broker refers a lender, say: "I have my own pre-approvals, but I am open to considering your lender. What exactly makes them the best fit for this specific deal?" This creates a win-win. The broker might earn their fee, and you might actually get a better interest rate with a faster underwriting team.

Secret #2: The Broker's Commission dictates the Seller's math.

Brokers typically charge a 10% commission of the total sales price, however, it is not uncommon for the percentage to decrease with larger transactions (the percentage usually decreases slightly as deal value increases).Why do you care what the broker makes? Because it helps you calculate the Seller's Net Proceeds. When you submit an offer, the Seller is not looking at your top-line number; they are looking at what they take home. If you offer $1,000,000, the Seller immediately deducts $100,000 for the broker, $200,000 for capital gains taxes, and $150,000 to pay off their remaining equipment loans.Suddenly, your $1,000,000 offer only puts $550,000 in their pocket. By understanding the fees and taxes hitting the Seller, you *can craft far more empathetic, creative offers, and you will finally understand why they fight so hard over a $25,000 counter-offer.*

Secret #3: I really dislike working with buyers who present themselves as "Private Equity."

As you already know, it drives me absolutely crazy when a buyer—who is clearly an individual or a husband-and-wife team—inquires about a small Main Street business using a fake "Investment Arm," "Holdings Company," or "Equity Partners" title.I don't know which online marketing guru is telling you to do this, but please stop. I automatically, and maybe unfairly assume you are going to be overly analytical, incredibly difficult, and treat a $750,000 plumbing company transaction like a $1 Billion hostile corporate takeover. Be authentic. Main Street sellers want to sell to real people, not faceless holding companies.

Secret #4: A lot of Brokers have no idea what they are doing.

The barrier to entry for becoming a business broker in many states is frighteningly low. You will encounter brokers who do not know how to read a P&L, who drastically overvalue businesses to win listings, and who give Sellers terrible legal advice. The Play: Be polite, but trust your own team. Rely on your CPA and your Attorney. Trust, but aggressively verify.

Secret #5: We do not want to get coffee with you.

I know we covered this in Chapter 3, but as we close this book, I need to say it one last time. Brokers receive daily requests from buyers wanting to buy us coffee so they can explain their search criteria.If I said yes to all of them, I would drink 14 extra cups of coffee a week. My job is to sell the listings I currently hold, not to act as your personal shopping assistant. And please, do not ask me to call you if a "$1M SDE, absentee-owned, zero-risk unicorn" hits the market. If that puppy shows up on my front porch, I am buying it myself. Be a sniper, define your realistic parameters, and come to me when you are ready to pull the trigger on a real-world asset.

Secret #6: The Multi-Bank Lending Truth

Just because one or two banks say no to your loan application, it does not mean the third lender won't say yes. Every bank has highly unique internal risk tolerances, credit appetites, and industry quotas. If a bank rejects your deal, do not blindly give up.However, do not be naive either. Treat a bank rejection as a free, professional diagnostic warning. Read their denial letter carefully and understand exactly why they said no. If one bank rejects you due to an internal policy against restaurants, keep pushing. But if five separate banks reject your application, pay attention. The market is giving you a definitive warning that there is a fundamental flaw with the transaction—likely an issue regarding an inflated valuation versus price, a complete lack of relevant buyer operational experience, an unstable deal structure, or structural industry decline.

Final Notes From The Lenders Desk

👁 Lenders Note #1: The SBA Lifeline vs. The Conventional Myth

Let's be completely honest: SBA loans exist because without that 75% government guarantee, banks would never consider financing small business acquisitions. While conventional commercial loans have fewer government hoops and paperwork guidelines, qualifying for one as a third-party, first-time buyer is nearly impossible. To even entertain a conventional acquisition loan, a bank will demand a significantly higher DSCR, deep industry-specific executive experience, a cash down payment of 20% to 30% minimum, and clean hard collateral to back the entire note. If you don't have a massive balance sheet, embrace the SBA process—it is your only viable path.

👁 Lenders Note #2: The LO Competency Gap

There is no universal certification or licensing exam required to become an SBA Loan Officer. The title on the business card does not equal expertise. There are active loan officers out there right now who literally do not know how to spread

business financial statements, and many who have never successfully closed a complex business acquisition. Do your due diligence on your banker.

👁 Lenders Note #3: The "Bad Deal" Litmus Test

When you interview a lender, ask them this exact question: *"Can you tell me about a deal of yours that went absolutely bad?"* Very few borrowers ever ask this. If you are talking to a loan officer who claims they've never had a loan default or a deal blow up in their face, you are talking to someone who hasn't been in this industry long enough to protect you. The greatest underwriting insights are forged in the deals that failed.

👁 Lenders Note #4: The 1% Referral Fee Secret

By law, an SBA lender can pay a referral fee to absolutely anyone who holds a valid US Tax ID—not just licensed business brokers. If you introduce a searcher to a lender, and that bank hasn't previously engaged with them, the bank will quietly pay a 1% referral fee on the funded loan amount upon closing.

👁 Lenders Note #5: Check Your Entitlement at the Door

Just because your target deal perfectly checks every abstract box in the official SBA standard operating procedures does not mean a bank is obligated to lend you millions of dollars. Lenders evaluate you as a human being from your very first email interaction. Of the traditional "5 Cs of Credit" (Capital, Capacity, Condition, Collateral, and Character), the most critical one is Character. No amount of perfect deal fundamentals can overcome an underwriting committee's doubts about a buyer's integrity or arrogance.

The Final Word

Buying a business is one of the most rewarding, life-changing financial decisions you can ever make. It is the ultimate shortcut to building true wealth and taking control of your own destiny.

But it is not a drive-thru window. It requires grit, discipline, and the willingness to look reality in the eye.

You will face moments of intense doubt during this process. You will lose deals you thought were guaranteed. You will spend money on due diligence only to find out a Seller was lying. You will get knocked down.

Consider those moments your training. Pay the tuition, learn the lesson, and get back up. The market is full of incredible, profitable, life-changing businesses waiting for a buyer with the discipline to find them and the courage to close them.

You have the vocabulary. You have the math. You have the playbook. Go win the fight!